Bournville – Then and

Cover: *The Courtyard Griffin's Brook House, circa 1909 and the same building in 2000 when being renovated. Renamed 'THE HOLDINGS' it now provides flats for single young people.*

To Margaret & Ron,

With many thanks.

Bournville
Then and Now

by

Margaret A. Broomfield

Margaret A. Broomfield (PEGGY)

William Sessions Limited
York, England

ISBN 1 85072 260 9

Printed in 11 on 12 point Plantin Typeface
by Sessions of York
The Ebor Press
York, England

Acknowledgements

I AM GREATLY INDEBTED to the following for giving me permission to quote from copyright and other sources:

Mr Roger Cadbury, Chairman, Bournville Village Trust, for extracts from various Bournville Village Trust publications.

Mr Ivor G. H. Cooke for information regarding the sale of The Woodlands Estate 1900 and Hole Farm.

M/s Sarah Foden, Manager of Information and Library Services, Cadbury Limited, for extracts from *Bournville Works Magazine*.

Mr Michael Harrison, for quotes and photographs from his book *Bournville – model village to garden suburb* published 1999.

The Executors of the late Miss G. Letitia Haynes, for extracts from her book *Old Hay Green Lane* being part of *Memories of a Bournville Child, 1920-1940*.

Dr R. J. Hetherington for his report on *The Roman Road between Gloucester and Birmingham north of the Lickey Hills*, printed in 1969 by the Oxford University Press in Transactions of the Birmingham Archaeological Society.

Dr Michael Hodder, Planning Archaeologist, Birmingham City Council, for extracts from an article, written by him and Mr Lawrence Barfield, in *Current Archaeology 78*.

Mrs N. M. Hopkins, Literature Secretary, The Northfield Society, for quotes from their sundry occasional papers.

Mrs Joan H. Jones, for material from *Maps of Birmingham*, written by her late husband, Mr John Morris Jones, ACP, FRGS, in 1975.

Miss Fiona Tait and others, Birmingham Central Library Archives Department.

I wish also to record my sincere thanks to those who have supplied me with written accounts and photographs relating to residences and farmsteads that were in the Bournville area at the beginning of the 20th century. They are:

Mr and Mrs Alan Chumbley, Mr Selby Clewer, Mrs Mary Collier, Mrs Kathleen Edwards, Mr David Gillett, Mrs Pauline Godsall, Mr Edward Harris, Mr Nicholas Holding, Mr Oscar Hopkins, Mrs Meriel Hunt, Mrs Margaret J. Lane, Mrs Sylvia Latham, Mr Ray Lucas, Mr George Parsons, Mr Michael Rymill, Mrs Joy Sadler and Mrs Anthea Richards, Mr Richard Seaman, Mrs Betty Sheward, Mrs Jean Smith of Northfield, Mrs Gillian Stokes, Mrs Rita Wallace and Mr Roger Wallbank.

I am grateful to all those who have encouraged me in my endeavours, particularly those who gave me addresses and telephone numbers of long lost acquaintances; without their help this book would not have been possible.

My final acknowledgement must go to Mrs Kate Wallbank who, despite having many commitments, has spent a great deal of time reading and correcting my manuscript. Her constructive criticism has, as ever, proved to be of immense value and I am greatly indebted to her.

* It is with regret I record the death of Mr Alan Chumbley and Mr Ivor Cooke. I am truly grateful to both these good people for the help and encouragement they gave me when I began to research the history of The Bournville Estate.

Contents

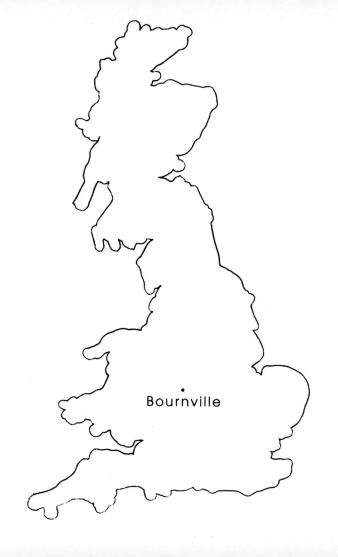

Bournville

*I dedicate this book to all those who,
like me, celebrate the centenary of
The Bournville Village Trust*

Foreword

THE NAME OF BOURNVILLE is renowned across the world. It is noted not only for the wonderful chocolate which is made at the Bournville factory of Cadbury, but also it is acknowledged for the important contribution of the Bournville Village Trust in the field of town planning. Laid out as a pre-eminent example of a garden city, thanks to the vision of George Cadbury, Bournville is a place which draws to it the praise of outsiders and the affections of those who live there. With its village green, ear-catching carillon, streams, playing fields and tree-lined roads, Bournville calls out to us a place which is embedded deeply within the city yet which still is bonded to a rural past.

But how many people who are pulled by the attractions of Bournville are aware of its history? And is it not true that most people feel that Bournville's past begins only with the opening of the Cadbury factory in 1879? Of course, Bournville has a history before chocolate production began and this is the great joy and lesson of this book by Margaret A. Broomfield. Margaret herself admits that it was a challenge to find out 'what was here prior to the Cadbury factory being built and the gradual growth of the Bournville Estate'. She has risen admirably to that challenge and with success she has drawn back the curtain of history and shown us the importance of rural Bournville to the modern neighbourhood.

Dr Carl Chinn

Introduction

THE PUBLICATION OF MY BOOK *A Bournville Assortment* in 1995 led to my receiving correspondence and telephone calls from friends, and folk hitherto unknown to me, saying how much they had appreciated reading a 'potted history' of the development of the Bournville Estate. One question raised was, 'what was here prior to the Cadbury factory being built and the gradual growth of the Bournville Estate?' This was a challenge and I decided to research books, maps and occasional papers in the hope of finding some clues. I am pleased to be able to put before you the result of my efforts. I have tried to give an account of the Midland Plateau area, as it might have been, from pre-history times to the present day. I hope the reader will be stimulated to study further the history of Bournville and its surrounding neighbours, namely Kings Norton, Northfield, Selly Oak and Weoley Castle.

In recent years it has been suggested that designated green belt areas should be used for housing and the like. Public reaction has been mixed. I think it is true to say the majority do not wish to lose yet more areas of natural beauty. But beware! It could happen. I therefore suggest you make written and pictorial records of what you see in your own locality as you go about your daily life, for in this day and age the transformation of a site can be undertaken in days. Next time you venture forth, the high-rise block of flats or office block may have been demolished in the same way that farm-buildings and picturesque cottages have vanished during the 20th century. Who would have imagined 50 years ago, that one day many parts of the Cadbury factory would be demolished and the site laid bare until the rise of 'Cadbury World'? Just think. In years to come your photograph could be invaluable to someone wanting to know how things were at the turn of the 21st century.

The Midland Plateau

IN HIS BOOK *Maps of Birmingham*, published in 1975, John Morris Jones one-time headmaster of George Dixon Junior School writes:

> The Midland Plateau has been isolated throughout history until recent times. It is far from the sea, accessible by small streams only, and was formerly surrounded and largely covered by dense deciduous jungle. While Low-land Britain was cleared and settled by successive invaders, only refugees of earlier cultures went to join the primitive hunters of Arden. It was not until later Saxon times that the Plateau was colonised and then by groups from earlier settlements. The bounding river valleys were important corridors of human movement, but the Plateau was always culturally poor. There was an abundance of game and fish, and some cultivable land, but most of Arden could not be tamed without great labour.

This theory was accepted until recently when, as a result of systematic searches of the banks of streams, several sites were recorded as being from the Bronze-age period. I will enlarge upon this later.

History books tell us of times, many thousands of years ago, when our predecessors would have lived in small family groups. They would have been hunters and gatherers, relying on crudely hewn stone implements and weapons in order to kill their prey not only for food, but also for the animal skins to make into tents and clothing. Folk are known to have lived in hillside caves in areas such as Kinver in Worcestershire.

Then came the ICE-AGE, followed by a much warmer climate. As a result, watercourses that had previously been small streams and rivulets became swollen rivers, and the lower ground was swamped. Consequently man moved to the higher ground. It is from all those years ago that we now have high-ways such as 'The Ridgeway' which runs south of Redditch in Worcestershire. As the ice receded it deposited rock that it had carried from the north. Could it be that some of these 'erratic deposits' were left in Bournville?

I am grateful to M/s Sarah Foden, Manager of Information and Library Services, Cadbury Limited, for giving me permission to quote the following from the November 1958 edition of *Bournville Works Magazine*.

The Bournville Boulders.

Doubtless there are those among us who have never heard of the Bournville Boulders, and they may be interested in the following account of their discovery and the various speculations concerning them. The story begins in the B.W.M. of January, 1906, in which the late J. S. Lancaster wrote an article on the famous 'Deepdale Boulder' of Shap granite found near Darlington. Although this boulder weighed about 30 tons, it had, said Mr. Lancaster, been swept along by a glacier, probably from Westmorland, during the Glacial period.

In the following issue, a lady, writing from Elm Road, Bournville, claimed that she had a glacier-borne boulder literally at her doorstep, although it was of a modest size, weighing a mere quarter-of-a-ton. As a matter of interest, we must record that this boulder has since been transported to Woodbrooke Road, and is now in the garden of Mr. and Mrs. G. Barnes.

Is it still there I wonder?

Again I quote from *Bournville Works Magazine* dated November 1958.

Bournville Memorial to Great Ice-Age.

When in December 1908 a large boulder was unearthed during excavations at Bournville, Professor Papworth, F.R.S., of Birmingham University, was asked to report on how it came here, its place of origin and its composition. He stated authoritatively that our boulder was a fine example of Arenig erratics, composed of volcanic ash, and had been brought down by ice during the glacial period. The professor, however, did not have the field to himself. Mr. Louis Barrow, Chief Engineer at Bournville in those days, held the view that since the boulder was found below the top level of the Keuper Marl, or original level of the Bournville ground, ours was no ordinary glacial boulder.

After much argumentative discussion, Professor Lapworth was prevailed upon to return to Bournville, survey our boulder anew and advance another theory. He was, however, adamant. He did not suggest for a moment that there had been cheating, but inferred that the boulder had been placed by the hand of man and not left by the ice in the remote past. Poking round the site with his umbrella, the professor unearthed from underneath the bed of the boulder, a very Victorian paving brick, and gravely asked Mr. Barrow if he felt that that too might be prehistoric! It was now agreed to agree with the expert. But the problem remained – if the boulder had been placed there by man, why was it done? And when?

A third witness now entered the inquiry. He was Mr. G. W. Brice, the Cashier, and he probably knew nothing whatever about Keuper Marl or the Ice Age, but he was, none the less, the man who knew why the boulder was where it was. Mr. Brice had come up with the Firm from Bridge Street in 1879, and he had a good memory. He recalled that when Bournville Lane had been widened years before, this particular boulder had been unearthed. Mr. Richard Cadbury thought that it would look well in his garden at Uffculme, and decided to have it removed. As, however, this proved too big a job, a trench was made and the boulder buried and forgotten.

The article goes on to say that in all 40 such boulders were unearthed in the district, with the *most recent being discovered during the excavations when Rowheath grounds were laid out in 1923.*

n.b. The Bournville boulders can be seen in Bournville Lane just to the west of the entrance to Bournville Station.

*Section of glacial deposits
exposed during excavations
at Cadbury Works,
Bournville (1938).*

*Ice-age boulder,
Bournville Lane.*

The Neolithic Period

BY THIS TIME man was wearing garments made from woollen cloth. He had discovered fire and had progressed to making a canoe by painstakingly carving out a fallen tree trunk. His tools were less crudely-made stone implements than those of his forefathers. He also used bone tools. By this time he had established that a dog was 'man's best friend' in that it was not just a companion but also would be a guard against would-be attackers and thieves.

Midland Plateau Settlements of the period are known to have been at BOURNE POOLE (Aldridge) and PACKINGTON nr. Coventry. ROUND BARROWS on the Clent hills are believed to date from this period.

We refer to the period from 1800BC to 500BC as the BRONZE AGE and we refer to the people living during the first part of that period as BEAKER FOLK. The name has come about as the result of many items of hand-fashioned geometrically ornamented drinking vessels of the time being found in burial mounds. We believe they were buried with the dead and would have contained food and drink. A fragment of one such artefact was unearthed near Overbury in Worcestershire in 1996 when the Channel 4 Television 'Time Team' archaeologists were being filmed there. During the 1950s and intermittently since, systematic searches along the banks of streams have been made and as a result layers of heat-shattered stones and charcoal have been found. I quote from an article written by Lawrence Barfield and Michael Hodder in *Current Archaeology 78* in 1981.

> A burnt mound survey in the south Birmingham area was begun by M. Nixon in the 1950s and this is now being continued by members of the Department of Ancient History and Archaeology of Birmingham University. The survey has so far located 15 sites in an area some 12 kms across between Northfield and Acocks Green, south of the Birmingham City

Centre. It can be suggested as a result of the survey that in the south Birmingham area these sites occur at intervals of about 2km. on all the minor streams while on some stretches the interval is less than 1km. In the wider area, bounded by the Rivers Trent, Stour, Avon, Blythe and Tame, a total of 30 sites is now known.

Burnt mounds are said to date from around 1200BC. Excavations of a burnt mound took place in Cob Lane, Bournville in the early 1980's. I quote again from *Current Archaeology* 1981.

> A first season of excavation was started last year on one of the Birmingham sites, at Cob Lane, Northfield, where there is a clear exposure in the bank of the Griffins Brook. Two tons of stone from this mound have so far been sieved and not a single bone or artefact has been recovered. The mound had been set at the very edge of the former stream channel and layers of burnt stones had spilled down into this channel. The lower levels of the old stream bed deposit were water-logged, preserving wood, hazelnut shells and beetles.

The article goes on to say that the site studied is considered unlikely to have been a permanent settlement site due to frequent flooding in the area.

It is suggested the mounds are the result of Bronze-age man burning large quantities of wood in order to generate intense heat and then piling stones on top to use either as a cooking device, or, by pouring water on to the heated stones, he would have created a type of sauna. To date, the latter seems the more likely possibility.

Those readers, who, like me, are avid viewers of Channel 4 Television's *Time Team* will have seen geophysicists walking the terrain with their recording equipment in order to gather resistance readings. This involves passing an electric current into the ground at measured intervals and where the ground is free-draining a reading of high resistance will be recorded. If the ground retains water it will record low resistance. Such a survey was undertaken fairly recently in Woodlands Park, Bournville, and showed the area of a mound which was visible in a stream bank. Prior to Burnt Mounds being found the only evidence for the Bronze-age period in Birmingham was a few Bronze-age axes.

During the SUB-BOREAL dry-warmer period which occurred around 1500BC the forests and swamps decreased. Those living from 900BC to 500BC are known to us as CELTS. They too settled on the hills and terraces of the area and made hill-forts for herding and defence purposes. Such places were CORNOVII, known to us as the Wrekin in Shropshire, and CORITANI at Leicester. BERRY MOUND was a hill-fort situated at Solihull Lodge. It covered an area of 11 acres and had a perimeter of approximately 655 metres. The hill-fort at WYCHBURY HILL on the Clent hills covered 7½ acres. CASTLE RING on Cannock Chase covered 12 acres. So this is how the Plateau was inhabited in pre-historic times. (Map 1.) Then came the ROMAN INVASION.

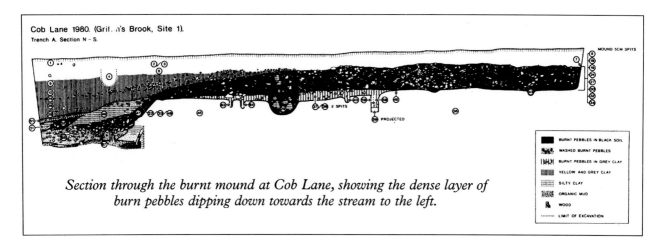

Cob Lane 1980. (Grif...n's Brook, Site 1).
Trench A. Section N – S.

MOUND 5CM SPITS

2 SPITS

PROJECTED

BURNT PEBBLES IN BLACK SOIL
WASHED BURNT PEBBLES
BURNT PEBBLES IN GREY CLAY
YELLOW AND GREY CLAY
SILTY CLAY
ORGANIC MUD
WOOD
LIMIT OF EXCAVATION

Section through the burnt mound at Cob Lane, showing the dense layer of burn pebbles dipping down towards the stream to the left.

Excavation of burnt mound at Cob Lane.

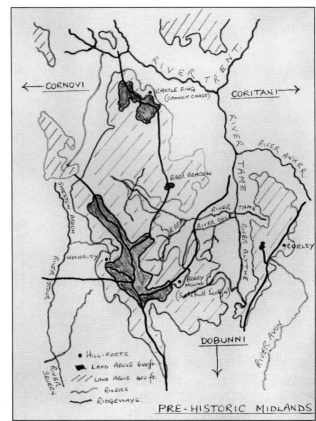

Map 1.

9

Roman Times

IN 43 AD Claudius and his army invaded Britain and made a base in London. From there his troops advanced, one column to the west, another to the north and two legions to the north-west. History books tell us they made slow but steady progress. As the soldiers marched forward, others would follow behind constructing roads as they went.

The FOSSE WAY, running from Cirencester to Leicester, was made in 47 AD. The Romans met very little national resistance, but there were some tribesmen based on the hill-forts. One Roman base was made at HIGH CROSS, prior to an advance across Cannock Chase and then on to the Wrekin in Shropshire, where the Roman legions won the day in 48 AD. As a result the conquerors built VIROCONIUM (Wroxeter).

Mention must be made here of the tremendous amount of work that has been done at Wroxeter in the past, and continues today, by archaeologists and historians of Birmingham University. For many decades they have painstakingly trowelled away layers of earth to expose mosaic flooring, fragments of Roman pottery and other artefacts. Year by year yet more interesting finds come to light and the area now gives us a clear sight of the lay-out of buildings. Recently the discovery of a Roman harbour in the area has been reported. One cannot help but realise just how advanced the Romans were in design and planning of buildings all those years ago.

We have all read books or been taught lessons about the straightness of the roads the Roman invaders made. There are two or three which run through the Midlands, notably WATLING STREET, part of which runs from Mancetter to Wroxeter (present day A5); RYKNIELD STREET, a highway running from Bourton-on-the-Water in the Cotswolds through to Weston Sub-edge on to Bidford-on-Avon, Studley, Forhill nr. Weatheroak, thence through Birmingham suburbs Lifford, Stirchley, Selly

Park, Bournbrook and Edgbaston (Metchley Camp), to Great Hampton Row/Wheeler Street, Sutton Park and thence to Derby and beyond, and a third which we believe runs from GLEVUM (Gloucester) to SALINAE (Droitwich) and on to METCHLEY, the only known Roman camp in the Midlands. METCHLEY is considered to be the oldest man-made structure in Birmingham. Established in AD46 it covered a 14½ acre site and is believed to have accommodated half a legion.

With reference to this third road, R. J. Hetherington and D. B. Whitehouse wrote an account of their findings when observing contractors' excavations near 53 Swarthmore Road, Weoley Hill in April 1963. The article was printed in *Transactions of the Birmingham Archaeological Society* Vol. 83, 1969, by Vivian Ridler at the Oxford University Press. I am indebted to Dr Hetherington for giving me permission to quote from that publication.

> The road called in recent years the upper Saltway from its use (attested in the Domesday book) for carrying salt northwards from Droitwich, has never had a known course in the City of Birmingham. It has always been obvious that the Bristol Road represents it, but this in its present form is almost entirely a product of the Turnpike Age and none of its straight stretches can be used as evidence. It is known, however, that from Selly Oak northwards, the medieval route left the present road near the University gates (see Ryknield Street).

It is therefore suggested that the Upper Saltway met Ryknield Street at Edgbaston Church. Again I quote from the Transactions of Birmingham Archaeological Society.

> No researcher, however, has been able to conduct the Upper Saltway from the Lickey Hills to Edgbaston Church. The evidence was insufficient. In the early 19th century 16 Roman coins were found at Pigeonhouse Hill, just south of Northfield, and of course, Metchley Camp lies near the presumptive route. Finally, a few years before 1939, when Harborne Bridge (taking Harborne Lane over the Dudley Canal) was rebuilt to accommodate the Outer Ring Road, a surveyor noticed what he took to be a section of Roman road exposed

in the corner of the allotment grounds north-east of the bridge. It was natural, therefore, to assume a line veering away from the Bristol Road somewhere between Northfield and St Mary's Church, Selly Oak, past Harborne Bridge and Metchley Camp to Edgbaston Church. With this in mind, following a discussion with D. B. Whitehouse at a meeting of the Northfield Survey Group, R. J. Hetherington undertook to watch all contractors' trenches in that area, which was then undergoing many building operations.

It would appear that nothing of note was found until the early 1960's when, and I quote yet again from the *Transactions of The Birmingham Archaeological Society,*

In 1963, a gravel bed was found sectioned by a storm-water drain on land being developed at Weoley Hill, far north of its expected position and running in an unexpected direction. West of the drain trench was visible a disused cart track with a small stream alongside (indeed, the drain had been cut to take this stream) and pre-1930 Ordnance maps show a straight line, north of Northfield Manor House and Middle Park Farm, which denotes this cart track and its stream, the latter running into the brook in Weoley Hill Parkway. Moreover, at the junction the brook itself formerly followed the line for a short time as if diverted by the road. Part of the stream still remains in a belt of spinney between Bryony Road and Swarthmore Road below Bryony House. After this observation had been checked and supplemented by excavation, further study of maps revealed that the line above continued further east, crossed Bristol Road by Westhill College and went on to meet Ryknield Street at Selly Park Recreation Ground.

The report goes on to say

If the Upper Saltway met Ryknield Street here, we have a road junction of the Roman period and a probable origin of the Domesday manor of ESCELAIE (Selly), whose manor house

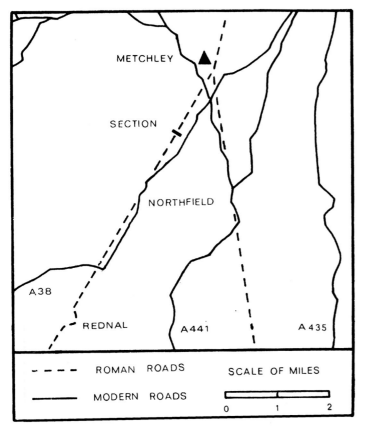

METCHLEY

▲

SECTION

NORTHFIELD

A38

REDNAL   A441   A435

- - - - ROMAN ROADS
———— MODERN ROADS

SCALE OF MILES

0   1   2

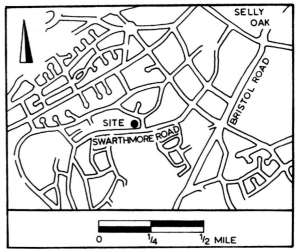

SELLY OAK

SITE ●
SWARTHMORE ROAD

BRISTOL ROAD

0   ¼   ½ MILE

Maps showing the Roman roads between the Lickey Hills and Birmingham, and the position of the section at Weoley Hill.

13

stood only a few yards away at the top of Bournbrook Road (though it is now re-erected at Bournville Village Green).

So we have evidence of a Roman Road once running through the middle of what is now the Bournville Estate.

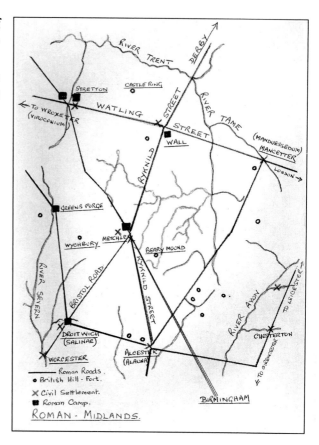

Anglo-Saxon Times

THE ANGLO-SAXON invasion of Britain took place in 449 AD with the ANGLES, a northern tribe from Schleswig in Germany, arriving in the Midlands via the rivers Humber, Trent and Tame. They were to rule East Anglia, Mercia and Northumberland.

The ANGLIAN KINGDOM of MERCIA with its capital at Tamworth covered an area south of the river Trent and it is estimated as being made up of small family groups or units totalling 5,000 households.

In the meantime the SAXONS, from what is now Holstein in Germany, made their way to the area via the rivers Severn and Avon and then by the Roman roads of the area. They established the kingdoms of Essex, Sussex and Wessex.

While all that was going on, the JUTES, also from Germany, were invading the south-eastern part of England and the Isle of Wight, establishing themselves in Kent and making Canterbury their capital.

It is thought the Angles settled on the Midland Plateau because of its well-drained south-facing slope with its light soil lending itself to easy ploughing. With plenty of clear never-failing springs running into streams there would have been fish and game in reasonable supply.

Materials for building, such as timber, sandstone, reeds and osiers were all near at hand. Wild hog and other animals would have foraged in the forests and game-birds would fly overhead providing plenty of sport for the hunter-gatherer and food for his family.

I have made mention of John Morris Jones's booklet *Maps of Birmingham* in a previous chapter, and I turn to it again now; Mr Jones lists the following names of local ANGLO-SAXON tribal groups:

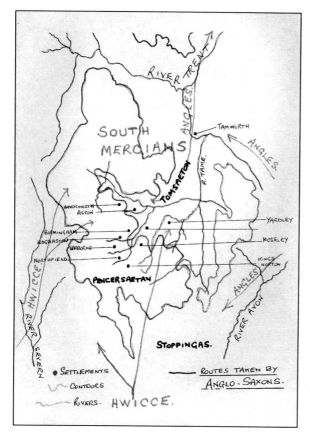

TOMSAETON	– Tame dwellers, probably included Birmingham, Aston and Edgbaston.
STOPPINGAS	– Arden, Wooton Wawen, Avon Valley.
PENCERSAETAN	– Bromsgrove, North Worcestershire.

It was during the ANGLO-SAXON administration that our country was cut up into sections and each part given the responsibility of governing its own administration of military affairs. The name given to these divisions at the time was 'Hundreds'. With the passage of time they have been called 'Shires', and are now referred to as 'Counties'.

Midland Hundreds were:

COLESHILL	– which includes Birmingham, Aston, Edgbaston, Bordesley, Bromwiches and Sutton.
CAME	– Northern Worcester, Kings Norton, Moseley and Northfield.

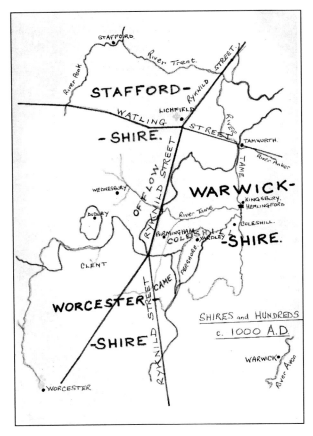

| PERSHORE | – Yardley, detached from Beoley and the rest of Abbey property. |
| OFFLOW | – South-east Stafford, Handsworth, Perry Barr, Harborne and Smethwick. |

About AD 630 a breakaway group of people, the HWICCE, formed an independent kingdom, with its capital at Worcester. They were an Anglian or maybe Anglo/British tribe who kept their own rulers for almost 100 years whilst at the same time acknowledging the supremacy of the Anglian kings of Mercia, a kingdom which covered the whole of the Midlands as far north as Lancashire. When the HWICCE became Christians a bishop was appointed to serve their kingdom and he set up the headquarters of his diocese at Worcester. The HWICCAN Kingdom included Northfield, Kings Norton and Yardley. By 1086 four settlements made up the Parish of Northfield. They were NORDFELD (Northfield), ESCELIE (Selley), BERCHELAI (Bartley) and west of Escelie lay another settlement referred to in the Domesday Book by the same name. (The Northfield Societies occasional paper no. 18 entitled *Discovering Northfield* states; 'There

17

can be little doubt that this was the settlement which was called Weleye in 1264, meaning 'a clearing where a heathen temple stood'. Under the pressure at the Domesday Inquiry, the clerk who made the entry probably became confused with the previous entry'.)

We have at last reached a point where place-names are familiar to us. Perhaps we can now begin to imagine how areas such as Selly Oak, Weoley, Northfield and Kings Norton looked all those years ago and how our forefathers worked and played in days past, when the area was devoid of the noise and hurly-burly of 20th-century life.

The Norman Conquest

WE ALL KNOW William of Normandy and his army invaded the coast of Sussex in 1066, and King Harold's army was defeated at Battle. William was duly crowned William I. The conquest took five years to complete. Many of those who followed William and survived the conflict had their allegiance rewarded with the gift of various English estates.

The Domesday Book of 1086 mentions Ansculf of Picquiny and his son, William. His stronghold at the time was Dudley Castle and he was awarded 30 manors that had been confiscated from the Earl of Mercia. Of these, 10 were in the Midland area. They were BARR, PERRY and HANDSWORTH (in the Offlow Hundred of Stafford), BIRMINGHAM, ASTON, WITTON, ERDINGTON, EDGBASTON (in the Offlow Hundred of Warwick) and NORTHFIELD and SELLY (in Worcester). Prior to the Norman Conquest SELLY had been the property of Ulwine, Shire-Reeve of Warwick.

Weoley was the centre of the Manor of Northfield. Its boundaries stretched from present day Pebble Mill eastwards through Dogpool to Rowheath, Wychall Farm and Turves Green in the south then north-westward to Kitwell, Bartley Green, Watery Lane, Mock Beggars Wood, and from there across the middle of Harborne reservoir and then north-easterly to the junction of Bristol Road and Edgbaston Park Road and so back to Pebble Mill.

Weoley Manor, owned by William Ansculf and said to be held by two Saxons, Tumi and Elva, covered an area of cultivated land together with woodland and a deer park. The building itself is thought to have been of mainly timber construction dating from 1150.

Records show that in 1264 Roger de Somery was granted a royal licence to build stone walls around the manor building as fortification. The buildings were enclosed by a moat between 1270 and 1280. Although long since drained, the depression of the moat can still be seen today, tho' sadly, due to

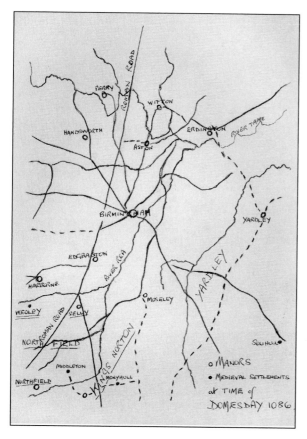

MANORS
MEDIEVAL SETTLEMENTS
at TIME of
DOMESDAY 1086

vandalism, Birmingham City Council, who are responsible for the site, have recently had to close it to the public.

It is believed the building was totally destroyed in 1380, possibly in order to enable a complete re-build. By 1650 the manor had fallen into dereliction. Story has it that in 1792 stones from the ruins were removed and used for other construction work. One possibility put forward is that some were used when the nearby canal was being constructed. We do know that unwanted bits of the original stonework were used to fill in the moat.

Throughout the years the manor's owners (see appendix) have been many and varied and their status/title altered through the centuries from feudal over-lord in Saxon times to landlord in the 19th century. By that date tenants were no longer men-at-arms but farmers and small-holders. It is suggested that the area must have been split into quite small pockets of land as the development of Northfield and Selly Oak got under way. From ordnance survey maps we learn that the area to the western side of Bristol Road from Selly Oak to Northfield was to remain as farmland until the middle of the 20th century. Such maps also give the names of farms and private houses of the time.

20

Manors of Greater Birmingham

MUCH HAS BEEN WRITTEN about the manors and part-manors which are situated in the area now covered by the City of Birmingham, and anyone who wishes to read up on the history of Manors such as Aston, Bordesley, Castle Bromwich, Edgbaston, Erdington, Handsworth, Harborne, Kings Norton, Northfield, Selly, Weoley, Perry Barr, Quinton, Sheldon, Witton and Yardley need only visit their local library for more information on the subject.

We are told they were all very similar during the Middle Ages, made up of fields and meadows, and an area of wasteland, together with small streams and the occasional pond, providing water for both human and animal consumption and a habitat for water fowl and other aquatic creatures. The Manor House was at the hub of the manor itself.

From the 15th century onwards quite a considerable change took place to the look of manor grounds with the enclosure of fields. Some pasture and arable common land was to survive until the Victorian period, by which time the main objective was self-sufficiency.

Waste land was cleared to make way for the rearing of sheep and in a short time such farming was recognised as a good source of income, being less labour intensive and with wool selling at a good price. During the autumn months cattle would be sold off for slaughter because of the lack of winter feed.

Was this then the way in which the land belonging to Weoley Manor was worked at the time? Did the land yield wheat, oats and root crops such as swede and turnips and was milk and its by-products (butter and cheese) plentiful or at least in good supply thus making the Manor self-sufficient? Did the harvesting of the various crops warrant a trip to Birmingham market? The answer is, we do not know. However, we do know that by the Georgian period the various manors were receiving

The Manor House – Northfield.

emigrants from the squalid and foul-smelling town areas, and as in all such migration it was the wealthy who moved first. Can we then, therefore, presume that it was as the result of such migration that we find larger type houses dotted about on the late Victorian maps of the area we are studying? Houses such as New House Farm, Woodbrooke, Belmont, The Davids, Griffins Brook House, Bournbrook Hall and The Dell. More of these later.

With the passing of time many such houses have been demolished to make way for modern buildings. New House Farm still exists, tho' now it is known as The Manor House. Situated just off the Bristol Road at Northfield it was, according to the Northfield Societies' publication 'Trade Directories', once the property of Joseph Gaskin 1841, then Frederick Isaac Welch, 1855. By 1865 reference is made to an Edward Baker and the name Manor House is given. In 1867 Messrs Chesshire and Gibson sold by auction *the Freehold Estate and Gentlemanly Residence, situate in the Parish of Northfield, in the County of Worcester.* The sale was held on August 22nd at *The Hen and*

Chickens Hotel, New Street, Birmingham. The Residence was described as *a substantially-built and comfortable residence having a southern aspect, with the Garden, Pleasure Grounds, Plantation and Orcharding.* The farm of the Freehold Estate for sale was known as *The New House Farm and consisted of a house and capital Homestead, eight fields of excellent meadow, arable, and pasture land, now in the occupation of S. Coley, as an annual tenant.* By 1876 the name of Francis Adkins is tied to The Manor House. The person referred to in 1888 is de Peyster Chance, and in 1894 the property was bought by George Cadbury.

The house and grounds remained the property of the Cadbury family until the death of Elizabeth M. Cadbury in 1951, when they were bequeathed to The University of Birmingham. Since then the house has undergone extensive alterations and is now a Hall of Residence for the University of Birmingham, and several small blocks of flats and houses have been built within the grounds, again to provide accommodation for students. The Manor Park, which consisted of old farm buildings, a barn, lake and children's play area, was handed over to the City of Birmingham at the same time.

Woodbrooke, once the residence of Frederick Elkington, silversmith, and later the first Bournville home of George and Elizabeth M. Cadbury has for many years been one of the Selly Oak Colleges.

In recent years Belmont, the one time residence of Mr Richard Bayliss, owner of Kings Norton Metal Company, was demolished to make way for Pocklington Place, a residential home for the visually impaired.

The Davids was for some years the property of George Jones, ironfounder until Laurence J. Cadbury, eldest son of George and Elizabeth M. Cadbury purchased it. It too was demolished to make way for the building of larger-type houses at the Wynds Point development in Hole Lane, Bournville.

All that is left to pin-point the site of Griffins Brook House (demolished about 1910/11) is the arched entrance to its courtyard and out-buildings, such as pig-stys, stables and tack-room, etc. For many years these premises were used by C. L. Holding and Sons, builders and joiners, as their Head office

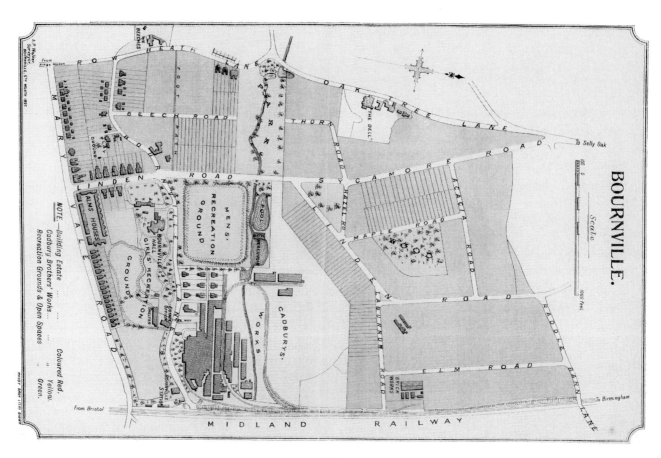

BOURNVILLE.

NOTE.—Building Estate ...... *Coloured Red.*
Cadbury Brothers' Works...... " *Yellow.*
Recreation Grounds & Open Spaces " *Green.*

A. P. Walker
Surveyor
BOURNVILLE. 5TH MONTH 1897.

To Selly Oak

To Birmingham

From Bristol

MIDLAND RAILWAY

24

Post Office and Shops, Sycamore Road, Bournville
(note the horse-drawn vehicle and lack of telephone kiosks).

and stock-yard. The firm closed a few years ago and, as I write, Bournville Village Trust are drawing up plans for the re-development of the site. Referring to the site as 'The Holdings' Bournville Village Trust *Outlook* winter 1999 reads:

It is hoped that the project will provide flats to help young people coming out of local authority care to make the transition to independence thus helping to reduce some of society's problems in the future, by helping to develop good, responsible citizens.

When George and Richard Cadbury brought their business to the area in 1879, Bournbrook Hall stood on a site now known as the Girls' Recreation Grounds in Bournville Lane. Bournbrook Hall and its grounds, the property of the Martin family, were purchased by the firm of Cadbury in 1893. In 1895 George Cadbury bought the remainder of the Bournbrook Hall Estate, 120 acres of land adjacent to the factory site. On it he built 143 houses which he sold at cost price, on a lease of 999 years for the ground on which they stood. This then was the beginning of The Bournville Estate.

Weoley Manor from 1536 to 1929

WEOLEY MANOR and its Estate became the property of the JERVOISE family in 1536 and was to remain so for almost 300 years when DANIEL LEDSAM purchased it in 1809. At this time the Manor was divided into three sub-manors, namely NORTHFIELD, SELLY and MIDDLETON.

Records tell us that on the 18th, 19th and 20th September 1820, Daniel Ledsam arranged for a large area of the Estate to be sold by auction. Referring to the Sale I am indebted to the Northfield Society for allowing me to quote the following from its Occasional Paper No. 12 entitled *Weoley Castle and its Families*, published 1981. It reads:

> A very extensive and desirable Estate comprising the Manor of Northfield and Weoley, the Advowson of the very valuable Rectory of Northfield and Cofton Hackett, together with divers farms and land containing together upwards of 2440 acres of land . . . in 94 LOTS. Of these LOTS, most were certain fields on various farms, but the Sale began with the seven large FARMS complete with FARMHOUSE and OUT-BUILDINGS including in most cases, BARNS and STABLE, COWSHED and FOLDYARD. The seven large FARMS were SELLY, NEW HOUSE, LODGE, WHITEHILL, SHENDLEY FIELD, SHENDLEY COURT and WEOLEY CASTLE FARM. In the case of NEW HOUSE FARM, the Residence was described as A MANSION with COACH-HOUSE.

The occasional paper goes on to record:

> LODGE FARM supported an acreage of 215½ of farmland consisting of 32 'inclosures' and was occupied by Charles Cooper by virtue of a lease dated 30th August 1805 for a term of 21 years at the yearly rent of £189.

SELLEY FARM, tenanted by John Lees, covered an area of 197½ acres, part under a lease expiring at Lady Day 1823 and the residue at Tenant at Will £235.15s.

WHITEHILL was farmed by William Willett and

SHENDLEY COURT by Thomas Green paying £107. annually.

SHENDLEY FIELD was occupied by James Whitehouse, holding 119½ acres for an annual payment of £117.

WEOLEY CASTLE FARM, tenanted by William Green, covered no less than 248 acres and commanded an annual rent of
£179.

A further 100 years were to pass before the remainder of the Estate was sold by James Goddington Ledsam's executors in 1929. The purchaser was the City of Birmingham and subsequently the last piece of rural Weoley became the Weoley Castle Housing Estate.

The Estate known as 'The Woodlands'

O N 20th JULY 1899 the Estate of John Abraham Esq., deceased, was sold by Grimley and Son at The Grand Hotel, Colmore Row, Birmingham. The Sales brochure states:

NORTHFIELD

About five miles from Birmingham

PARTICULARS PLANS AND VIEWS

of an important

FREEHOLD

Residential and building Estate

comprising a most substantially-built and handsome, medium sized

MANSION HOUSE

known as

'THE WOODLANDS'

including upwards of 27a. 2r. 13p.

of PLEASURE GROUNDS AND OLD TURF LAND.

BUILDING ESTATE

of about 195 acres

'MIDDLETON HALL FARM' 'HAY GREEN FARM' and 'THE HOLE FARM'

To be sold by auction (by direction of the Executors of the late John Abraham Esq.).

The Plan accompanying the sales brochure places the Estate in Northfield, Worcestershire.

Messrs Grimley and Son. Auctioneers, Surveyors and Land Agents had offices at 39-40 Temple Street, Birmingham.

Messrs Beale and Co. of 12 Newhall Street and Messrs Lane, Clutterbuck and Co. of 10 Temple Row were the Solicitors involved in the Sale.

The brochure was printed by Moody Brothers, Needless Alley and Fore Street, Birmingham.

With regard to 'The Hole Farm' the following is added.

> Through which a new road, called Woodlands Park Road, has recently been constructed in accordance with the requirements of the Local Authorities, including two good Residences and twelve Cottages, which will be offered in advantageous LOTS.

Further details of the Estate are as follows.

> The Estate has valuable frontage to Bristol Road, at Griffins Hill, not far from Selly Oak, and a long frontage to the road in continuation of Middleton Hall road, leading to Northfield Village and Railway Station, and also frontages of about 2,162 yards to Woodlands Park road; also frontages to Oak Tree Lane [*now the northern end of Selly Oak road*] Cob's Lane, Hole Farm Road, [*now Hole Lane*] and Hay Green road, [*now Hay Green Lane*]. It is pleasantly undulating, and from many points possesses charming views of diversified character. It was the intention of the late Mr. Abraham, had he lived longer, to develop the whole Estate for Building purposes. With this object, the new road has been constructed, which forms a direct connection between Middleton Hall Road and Bristol Road, and considerably shortens the route between King's Norton and Griffin's Hill. The extensive road frontages to the Estate is an element of great value, and it will not be necessary to construct many intersecting roads for further development.

The estate was situated on one side equi-distant from King's Norton and Northfield Railway Stations, and on the other, five miles from Birmingham, on the main Bristol Road, 1½ miles from Selly Oak, and adjoined the properties of Thos. S. Stock Esq. J.P., The Northfield Glebe, George Cadbury Esq. J. P., T. R. Bayliss Esq. J.P., Messrs Moore, and Mr Bentley.

Particulars of the various LOTS, numbering 15 in all, are as follows.

LOT 1. A valuable plot of FREEHOLD BUILDING LAND, having frontages to Oak Tree Lane and Hay Green Road adjoining land of George Cadbury Esq. and opposite the Bournville Estate, containing an area of 7 acres 1 rod 14 poles, quite ripe for the erection of artisans' dwellings.

LOT 2. Six FREEHOLD COTTAGES and GARDENS in Hay Green Road with the outbuilding thereto, in the occupation of Messrs Allen, Peach, Eaton, Sherwood, Dolby and Cooper at weekly rents amounting to £66.19s.0d. per annum.
Area of land: 1,523 sq. yards or thereabouts.
[*I believe these cottages are now nos. 59–69 Hay Green Lane.*]

LOT 3. A FREEHOLD GROUND RENT of £4. 3s. 0d. per annum, amply secured by two newly erected DWELLING HOUSES in Oak Tree Lane with the reversion-in-Fee in 1997.
[*Possibly 38 and 38a Selly Oak Road.*]

LOT 4. A FREEHOLD GROUND RENT of £22. 17s. 3d. per annum secured by 3,658 sq. yards of land, at the corner of Oak Tree Lane and Hay Green Road, leased to Mr. T. Halward for a term of 99 years from 25th March 1899 with the reversion-in-Fee.

LOT 5. HAY GREEN FARM
A small FREEHOLD FARM comprising a DWELLING HOUSE, HOMESTEAD, GARDEN and three ENCLOSURES of good sound LAND, having long frontages to Cob's Lane, and Hay Green Road, containing 13 acres 0 rods 9 poles, and available

for dividing into Building Plots. The HOUSE contains Entrance Hall, Parlour, Sitting-room, two Kitchens, Scullery, Brew-house, Pantry, two good Dairies, Cellar, five Bedrooms, and Cheese room.

The FARM BUILDINGS consist of Cowhouses for ten cows, Open Feeding Sheds, Stabling for six horses, with Lofts, Barn, Workshop, Granary, Fodder-house, Calf-pen, Piggeries and other Outbuildings.

Name of fields: ORCHARD,
                 COLTS HOVEL.
                 LITTLE MEADOW.
                 LONG CROFT.

The above is held by Mr. J. Oxenham, with other Lands, upon an annual tenancy, and for the purpose of this Sale the rent of this LOT shall be apportioned at £60 per annum.

LOT 6. A field of OLD TURF LAND, having a frontage to Hay Green Road and a frontage to a road leading from Griffins Brook to Bristol Road, containing 10 acres 0 rods 10 poles, adjoining property belonging to T. R. Bayliss. Esq., and quite ripe for building purposes. Apportioned Tithe Rent £1. 13s. 10d.
[*The above is the area of present day Hay Green Lane, Cobs Field, Cob Lane, Griffins Brook Lane, and the site of the Serbian Orthodox Church of St. Lazar.*]

LOT 7. A substantially-built FREEHOLD PROPERTY, consisting of six well-arranged DWELLING HOUSES, with out-offices and Gardens thereto, in Cob's Lane, near the corner of Hay Green Road in the respective occupation of Messrs Cutler, Barratt, Shepherd, Guest, Fesey, and Molesworth, as weekly tenants at rents amounting to £95. 12s. 0d. per annum.
Area 2,171 sq. yards.
[*Likely to be nos. 145 to 155 Cob Lane today.*]

LOT 8. THE WOODLANDS

A valuable FREEHOLD RESIDENTIAL ESTATE at NORTHFIELD having a frontage to Bristol Road of about 432 yards.

With LODGE at ENTRANCE GATE, excellent STABLING, CARRIAGE-HOUSES, GLASS-HOUSES, PLEASURE GROUNDS, LAWNS, GARDENS and ORCHARD, together with convenient FARM BUILDINGS, five fields of OLD TURF LAND and FISH PONDS, containing in the whole 27 acres 2 rods and 13 poles.

It is most substantially built and has an exceedingly attractive classic elevation in Brick Stucco, with Freestone Facing: it is placed well back from the road and protected by an Ornamental Fence Wall, and is approached by a CARRIAGE DRIVE, belted by fine grown FLOWERING and other SHRUBS of mature growth, and containing the following accommodation.

On the ground floor – approached by a Flight of steps, imposing Portico Entrance, spacious Hall; DINING-ROOM, 30ft. by 18ft; DRAWING-ROOM, 29ft. by 18ft. BOUDOIR; LIBRARY, 19ft. by 16ft. MORNING-ROOM, 24ft. by 15ft; and handsome Inner or Staircase Hall.

The Domestic portion, well screened from the Reception Rooms, includes:- SERVANTS' HALL 18ft. by 14ft; COOKING KITCHEN, 18ft. by 15ft. HOUSE-KEEPER'S ROOM, 17ft. by 11ft. Large BUTLER'S PANTRY COOK'S and STORE PANTRIES; SCULLERY, and Back Staircase. In the half-Basement Storey are; LAUNDRY, 29ft.6ins. by 17ft.6ins. Wine, Ale and Store Cellars, Larder, Dairy, Wash-house, Heating Chamber, W.C. and Ash-place; an approach to this Floor being arranged from the Ground level from the Yard.

On the Chamber Floor; spacious Landing and Corridors, eleven excellent Bedrooms, Dressing Room, two Bathrooms, two W.C.'s, Linen Closet, Housemaid's Closet, and back stairs, a well-lighted Billiard Room 24ft. by 18ft, and on the second floor a large Attic.

In an ENCLOSED PAVED COURT-YARD are well-arranged STABLE BUILD-INGS consisting of Two STABLES of three STALLS each, two LOOSE-BOXES, SADDLE ROOM (with stores over), two CARRIAGE HOUSES (with men's Living Rooms over), and an extensive Range of Lofts, in three divisions.

The OTHER OUT-BUILDINGS include:– Fowl-house, Piggeries, Fowl-pens (with netted runs), Boiler shed, two coal sheds, Brick-built Pump and Engine House (with deep well) two Potting Houses, and Open Timber Shedding.

The GLASS HOUSES, which have been ornamentally constructed in a first-class manner on the most approved modern principles, comprise CONSERVATORY 28ft. by 14ft: PLANT HOUSE, 26ft. by 12ft: STOVE HOUSE, 22ft. 6ins. by 20ft: two VINERIES, 56ft. x 20ft, and FORCING HOUSE, all heated by Hot Water Apparatus from one Boiler: COLD FRAMES etc.

THE FARMERY

Consists of a substantial, recently erected modern range of FARM BUILDINGS, comprising four-stall STABLE and LOOSE-BOX with LOFT over, HARNESS ROOM (with GRATE, FURNACE, and SINK) and an OPEN TILED ROOF CART SHED. A Timber-Built erection, comprising COW-HOUSE, with standing for five cows, having loft over; LARGE PIGSTYE, with loft over, COW-HOUSE, with standing for eight cows, having feeding passage behind Stalls; CHAFF-CUTTING HOUSE and OPEN FEEDING PENS.

This FINE RESIDENTIAL PROPERTY is enclosed by a Ring Fence, is studded with handsome Forest Trees and forms one of the most delightful Residences in the neighbourhood of Birmingham, from whence it is distant about five miles, and about a mile and a half from Northfield Station. The House stands about 550ft. above sea level, and the salubrity of the air is proverbial. The rides and drives in the surrounding district are noted for their beauty, and the Lickey Hills are within 3 miles. Apportioned Tithe Rent Charge £4 14s. 3d.

Names of fields.   HOUSE MEADOW.   THE WELCHES.   TOP FIELD.

THE LEYS.   BOTTOM FIELD.

LOT 9.   Two fields of OLD TURF, having a long frontage to HOLE FARM ROAD, forming a small BUILDING ESTATE which is quite ripe for development, adjoining the Grounds of 'THE DAVIDS' and abutting upon the grounds of 'THE WOODLANDS'; containing in the whole 12 acres 2 rods and 39 poles.
Apportioned Tithe Rent Charge £2 15s. 2d.
Field names.   FIRST HANCK'S
HANCK'S MEADOW.

LOT 10. A DETACHED RESIDENCE known as 'THE HOLE FARM HOUSE' with convenient FARM BUILDINGS and two enclosures of PASTURE LAND with a considerable frontage to HOLE FARM ROAD and forming a desirable small RESIDENTIAL ESTATE.
Apportioned Tithe Rent Charge £1 13s. 10d.
Names of Fields.   PADDOCK
SHOULDER of MUTTON
LOWER HURTS

The HOUSE contains Entrance Hall, Dining Room, Drawing Room, large Kitchen and Range, Baking Oven, Scullery, Dairy. On the First Floor, four good Bedrooms, Dressing Room, W.C. Principal Laundry and Back Stairs. On the Second Floor, two large Bedrooms. In the Basement are two Cellars. The Out-buildings comprise Wash-house, Coal-shed, Tool-house, Closet etc.

The FARM BUILDINGS comprise Coach-house, Two-stall stable, Piggeries, Fowl-house, Pigeon-cote; another Stable with loft, Cart-shed, Cow-house and large Barn with Bay

The House, Farm buildings and Enclosures are in tenure of Mrs Garland, at rents amounting to £57 per annum.

LOT 11. Four enclosures of OLD TURF LAND, having a long frontage to HOLE FARM ROAD and forming excellent SITES and RESIDENCES, containing together 9acres 1rod 5poles.

Apportioned TITHE RENT CHARGE £1. 16s. 0d.

Name of fields. LONG GROUNDS
                 UPPER HURTS.
                 BUMBERY MEADOW
                 BUMBLEBEE PARK.

The above land has a pleasant slope and is admirably suited for the erection of Villas.

LOT 12. Four enclosures of sound PASTURE LAND, having extensive frontages to HAY GREEN ROAD, HOLE FARM ROAD and the New Road called WOODLANDS PARK ROAD, containing together 24 acres 0 rods 38 poles, forming a very compact small BUILDING ESTATE, quite ripe for development.

Names of fields. FAR FINCH FIELD
                        NEAR FINCH FIELD.
                        THE THREE ACRES.
                        TAYLOR'S FIELD.
Apportioned Tithe Rent Charge £4 6s. 6d.

LOT 13. MIDDLETON HALL ESTATE.

Several enclosures of OLD TURF LAND, having extensive frontages to MIDDLETON HALL ROAD, HOLE FARM ROAD and the new road called WOODLANDS PARK ROAD, containing together 48 acres 1 rod 29 poles, forming a most eligible BUILDING ESTATE, quite ripe for development.

Name of fields *THE FIELD
                part of WHETSTONE MEADOW
                PIGSTY MEADOW
                part of HAY GREEN CLOSE
                *SWAIN'S PARK
                part of BIG WOOD
                *MUD PIECE
                OVER MEADOW
                *WINDMILL HILL
                part of POOL CLOSE.

The Field, Swain's Park, Mud Piece, and Windmill Hill are held by Mr J. Oxenham, with other lands, on an annual tenancy and for the purpose of this Sale the rent shall be apportioned at £74 per annum.

NOTE The Purchaser of this Lot shall give up part of Windmill Hill, for the purpose of continuing HOLE FARM ROAD as shown upon plan, if called upon to do so by the Local Authorities or by Mr T. Bayliss at any time within three years from the date of conveyance to such Purchaser.

LOT 14. HAY GREEN ROAD

Three enclosures of MEADOW LAND, having long frontages to HAY GREEN ROAD opposite HAY GREEN FARM HOUSE, and to a newly made road called WOODLANDS PARK ROAD, containing 14 acres 3 rods 37 poles, together with a BARN and other FARM BUILDINGS thereon, quite ripe for Building purposes, adjoining Property belonging to Messrs Moore.

Name of fields LONG MEADOW
RICK YARD
CROSS PIECE
ENCLOSURE.

Apportioned Tithe Rent Charge £2.4s.11d.

The above lands are in tenure of Mr J. Oxenham as a yearly tenant with HAY GREEN FARM, and for the purpose of this Sale the rent of this LOT shall be apportioned at £36 per annum.

LOT 15. WOODLANDS PARK ROAD BUILDING ESTATE

A FREEHOLD BUILDING ESTATE of 46 acres 1 rod 6 poles having a frontage to NORTHFIELD ROAD and to a new road called WOODLANDS PARK ROAD, comprising Enclosures of sound PASTURE LAND.

This LAND is situate close to MIDDLETON HALL ROAD, and about 10 minutes' walk from Kings Norton Railway Station, and is most admirably adapted for the erection of DWELLING HOUSES, suitable for the neighbourhood.

Name of fields part of WHETSTONE MEADOW
part of HAY GREEN CLOSE
part of BIG WOOD
NEAR LADY FIELD
part of POOL CLOSE.

Apportioned Tithe Rent Charge £10 1s. 3d.

Addendum

As an addendum to all the previous information, I would like to give my own interpretation as to where each individual LOT was in relation to present day landscape, and also to make clear that when HOLE FARM ROAD is mentioned this was where we now have HOLE LANE, HAY GREEN ROAD is now called HAY GREEN LANE, and the section of OAK TREE LANE referred to in LOT 1 is now the northern end of SELLY OAK ROAD.

LOT 1. Selly Oak Road / Hay Green Lane to Cedar Close and Cedar Road along the pathway that runs adjacent to 'The Beeches'.

LOT 2. Old houses, possibly 59 to 69 Hay Green Lane.

LOT 3. Possibly nos. 34 and 36 Selly Oak Road.

LOT 4. Nos. 2 to 8 Selly Oak Road and 1 and 3 Hay Green Lane.

LOT 5. Hay Green Lane, Bournville Lane, Cob Lane, Old Barn Road and Griffins Brook Lane.

LOT 6. Western end of Hay Green Lane, Hole Lane, western end of Griffins Brook Lane, Cob Lane.

LOT 7. Old houses in Cob Lane at the corner of Hay Green Lane.

LOT 8. The Royal Orthopaedic Hospital 'The Woodlands', Bristol Road, part of Hole Lane to Jervoise Drive and westerly to St Laurence Road.

LOT 9. Hole Lane from Jervoise Drive to Hole Farm Road.

LOT 10. Hole Lane from Hole Farm Road to eastern end of Heath Road South.

LOT 11. Hole Lane from eastern end of Heath Road South to Innage Road.

LOT 12. Land from Hole Lane in the west to Woodlands Park Road in the east and Hay Green Lane in the north to the footpath running adjacent to the rear of the flats in Mulberry Road.

LOT 13. From the footpath at the rear of the Mulberry Road flats, south-west to Middleton Hall Road and from Hole Lane in the west to Woodlands Park Road in the east.

LOT 14. Hay Green Lane, Woodlands Park Road, Mulberry Road area.

LOT 15. Roughly Northfield Road, Woodlands Park Road, Heath Road and Hawthorne Road area.

n.b. Directions are approximate.

FARMSTEADS *and* OTHER RESIDENCES
of the area in the 19th century

DURING THE 19th CENTURY, many owners of businesses based in the city centres began to move out to the surrounding countryside, and either bought existing residences or had homes built to their own design. Thus it was in the Bournville area, tho' the name Bournville did not materialise until 1879.

We know of some of the fine country houses of the area and I mention a few.

Selly Wood

Once the home of Edward Fereday, followed by John Worthington, retired wool merchant. Later it was the home of Kenneth J. Wilson, J.P., and his wife Mary Isobel and family, and then Christopher B. and Hannah H. Taylor occupied it and watched their family grow up there.

Selly Wood, c. 1965.

The Garden, Selly Wood, c.1965.

During the Second World War, part of the building was used by Friends' Relief Service as offices. Later it was demolished to make way for Selly Wood House, a full-care home for the elderly, and Queen Mother Court, sheltered housing for retired members of the teaching profession. Both are situated in Selly Wood Road. Residents of Queen Mother Court can look out on to much of the original garden – a joy to behold.

Westholme

This house was situated in Oak Tree Lane very near the corner of Hoyland Way. For many years it was the residence of Edward and Dorothy Cadbury, followed by Henry T. and Lucy Cadbury and their family. Later it was the home of Nicholas and Ruth Gillett and their children. Ruth Gillett was a daughter of Henry and Lucy Cadbury.

In the late 50's and early 60's part of the building was used by 'The Ockenden Venture' (now known as 'Okenden International'), as a hostel for young displaced East European teenagers. It too was demolished to make way for the re-development of the area.

41

Woodbrooke

A building standing a little way back from the Bristol Road at the foot of Griffin's Hill, it was once the residence of Geo. Elkington, silversmith, and in 1881 it was purchased by George Cadbury. He and his first wife, Mary, and their family lived there and, sadly,

Westholme, c.1950's.

Mary died there in 1887, leaving five young children. In 1888 George Cadbury married his second wife, Elizabeth Mary, and there were six children of the union. They moved to the Manor House at Northfield in 1894. Woodbrooke was temporarily in other occupation, but before long, George Cadbury decided it should be handed over to the Society of Friends as a college for men and women. It can still be seen today and is one of the Selly Oak Colleges.

Woodbrooke.

The Woodlands Mansion

The residence of Thomas Tipping Lawden, button manufacturer, in 1865 and later purchased by John Abraham (see previous reference).

Belmont

The property of T. Richard Bayliss, owner of Kings Norton Metal Company, in the early 1900's, this building stood on a site near the corner of Bristol Road and Hole Lane until it was demolished in recent years. It was replaced by Pocklington Place, a home for the visually impaired.

The Davids

This building stood in Hole Lane a few hundred yards away from the Bristol Road. Bentley's Worcestershire Directory for 1841 records a Mr. Middlemore living at 'The Davids'. He was followed by George Jones, ironfounder, a widower with one daughter, and household staff.

For many years this residence was the home of Laurence and Joyce Cadbury and their family. Following the death of Joyce Cadbury it was targeted by vandals and was subsequently partly destroyed by fire before being demolished. The Wynds Point development now occupies the site.

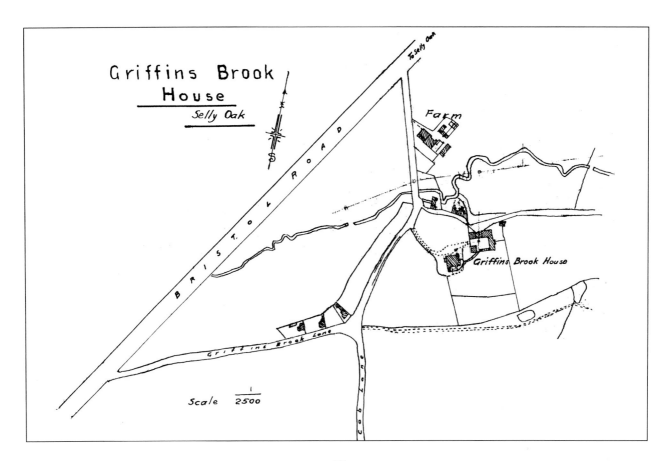

Griffins Brook House

Selly Oak

To Selly Oak

BRISTOL ROAD

Farm

Griffins Brook House

Griffins Brook Lane

Cob Lane

Scale $\frac{1}{2500}$

Griffin's Brook House.
A pen and ink drawing by Graham F. Carley.

46

Griffin's Brook House

This once imposing building stood on land owned by a Lawrence Lawrence Esq. It covered an area of 21 rods 2 poles and 37 perches. Miss G. Letitia Haynes in her book *A New Home in a Model Village* writes the following.

The Gateway, Griffin's Brook House, c.1909.

A rather derelict big country house, belonging to Mr. Lawrence with stabling, coach-houses, Chinese pagoda in the garden, and approached from the back by an overgrown track leading to the cottages in the adjacent lane. This track was so still and sinister, and so dark with overhanging trees, it was believed to be haunted. In these trees the rooks nested in number. They flew out to forage in the early morning with sturdy cawing and vigorous flight, and returned slow and heavy, with a subdued and weary call in the evening, to their nests in the tall trees.

Griffin's Hill

No longer in evidence, this was once the residence of Thomas Hancox, Sheriff's Officer.

Oak's Cottage, Griffin's Hill

No longer in evidence, was once the property of John Fallows, architect and auctioneer.

In addition to the larger houses already mentioned we know of a handful of cottages and several farmsteads in the area, most of which have long since gone. However some do still remain. To this day there are two semi-detached two-bedroom cottages still habitable and they are believed to date from 1684. They can be seen in Cob Lane (near the Police Station) which was, at one time, part of the Birmingham to Bristol highway. What tales those dwellings could tell us!

The Courtyard, Griffin's Brook House.

Thomas Quinney, 1853-1947, wrote his memoirs for the Northfield Mens' Adult School in 1943 when he himself was 90. In 1868 he lived at Longbridge Farm and he recalled the only transport available between Birmingham and Bromsgrove being the stage-coach which ran three times a week. The fare was 1/- return and with an agricultural worker earning between 10/- and 14/- per week, with the rent for his cottage being around 3/- per week, one can presume a journey to Birmingham by stage-coach was seldom, if ever, taken by the working class.

The Northfield Society Occasional Paper on 'Trade Directories' makes mention of a James Halward and a Benjamin Walker both of whom were boot and shoe makers and lived in Griffins Brook Lane. From the little knowledge I have of the area, I wonder whether one or other of these gentlemen ever lived at 'Rose Cottage', Griffins Brook Lane. The reason I remember this particular cottage so clearly is because when it was being razed to the ground, to make way for the present day bungalows on the site in the 50's, my father begged the little wrought-iron gate from its entrance. The reason my father wanted it? He and my mother had spent many hours courting in the area and had dreamt of living in Rose Cottage one day. They just wanted a memento. His plea was answered and the little gate was duly hung in a cotswold-stone wall my father built to divide the small orchard from the rest of my parent's garden at 102 Linden Road. As far as I know it is still there.

Another very old dwelling in the area which is still lived in is Park Cottage. Now no. 98 Weoley Park Road it was at one time part of Park Farm which was situated where St Andrew's Hall now stands.

Not so very many years ago, there were several farms in the Bournville area. They were FIVE GATES FARM, situated in the vicinity of Willow Road and Elm Road; BOURNBROOK FARM, sometimes referred to as FROGGATT'S FARM, situated in Bournville Lane / Linden Road area. YEW TREE COTTAGE FARM, Oak Tree Lane below Woodbrooke Road; WOODBROOKE FARM, the site of the present day West Midlands Police Station at the corner of Bristol Road and Bournville Lane. WALKER'S FARM, in the vicinity of Griffins BROOK CLOSE and Griffins Brook Lane.

SHEWARD'S FARM, at the corner of Hay Green Lane and Old Barn Road. ROWHEATH FARM at the southern end of Selly Oak Road, MIDDLETON HALL FARM, Woodlands Park Road / Bunbury Road area. STREET FARM stood where the present YMCA Bunbury Road, Northfield, is sited. WHITEHILL or PARK FARM, Whitehill Lane; MIDDLE PARK FARM occupied the site between Bristol Road and Swarthmore Road where we now have Bournville College.

In addition there were SHENLEY COURT FARM, situated near the corner of Shenley Fields Road and Shenley Lane, UPPER SHENLEY, at Shenley Hill.

YEW TREE FARM, Long Mynd Road / Spiceland Road area and LOWER SHENLEY, the site of St David's Church and Shenley Shopping Centre. I will refer to these farms in more detail in a future chapter. This then gives some idea of how the area looked when George Cadbury decided, in 1900, to set up a Trust which we now know as 'The Bournville Village Trust'.

Cottage at Cob/Griffin's Brook Lanes. Demolished late 50's.

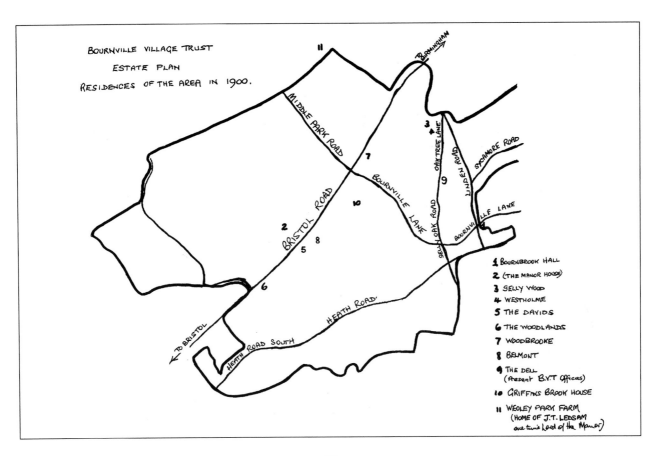

BOURNVILLE VILLAGE TRUST
    ESTATE PLAN
RESIDENCES OF THE AREA IN 1900.

TO BIRMINGHAM

MIDDLE PARK ROAD

BRISTOL ROAD

BOURNVILLE LANE

OAK TREE LANE

SELLY OAK ROAD

LINDEN ROAD

SYCAMORE ROAD

BOURNVILLE LANE

HEATH ROAD

TO BRISTOL

HEATH ROAD SOUTH

1 BOURNBROOK HALL
2 (THE MANOR HOUSE)
3 SELLY WOOD
4 WESTHOLME
5 THE DAVIDS
6 THE WOODLANDS
7 WOODBROOKE
8 BELMONT
9 THE DELL
   (Present B.V.T Offices)
10 GRIFFINS BROOK HOUSE
11 WEOLEY PARK FARM
   (HOME OF J.T. LEDSAM
   one time Lord of the Manor)

51

The Formation of Bournville Village Trust

THE FOLLOWING is an extract from my book *A Bournville Assortment* published in 1995.

In 1900 George Cadbury made it known that he did not wish to be a landlord and so, by placing in their charge 330 acres of land and 313 houses, valued at £172,000 he nominated 12 members of his family to be trustees.

The Trust Deed is dated 14th December 1900.

I have in my possession a booklet *The Bournville Village Trust,* dated 1901. The opening paragraph reads:

> The Founder is desirous of alleviating the evils which arise from insanitary and insufficient accommodation supplied to large numbers of the working classes, and of securing to workers in factories some of the advantages of outdoor village life, with opportunities for the natural and healthful occupation of cultivating the soil. The object is declared to be the amelioration of the condition of the working class and labouring population in and around Birmingham, and elsewhere in Great Britain, by the provision of improved dwellings, with gardens and open spaces to be enjoyed therewith.

The then Secretary to the Trust, John H. Barlow, continues to write thus:

> Briefly stated, the steps by which the Founder was led to recognise the necessity for some such scheme are as follows. The overcrowding in the poor insanitary districts of our large cities results, inevitably, in serious moral and physical deterioration. Shut up in dirty, evil-smelling streets and courts, deprived of fresh air and sunshine, strangers

to the sight of grass and flowers and trees, without means of healthy recreation, familiarised with evil from early child-hood, and surrounded by vice and temptation on every hand; what wonder if, while some bravely battle against and rise superior to their surroundings, an immense number are broken down by them and go to swell the terrible mass of vicious criminal and diseased humanity which is a disgrace and menace to our country!

Both the character and the physique of our population suffers, and it becomes increasingly manifest that if we are to hold our own in the rivalry of Nations it is imperative that a remedy be found. These facts are, of course, open to all, but they were specially impressed on the mind of the Founder through his association with the working men of Birmingham. For more than 40 years he has been Teacher of a men's Bible Class, going into Birmingham every Sunday morning for this purpose. In this way he has learned to know the life histories, and struggles of hundreds of men, and in the efforts to help them to a better life has again and again encountered the barriers caused by their surroundings. He set himself resolutely to face this difficulty, and the most hopeful solution that presented itself, was to give an opportunity for the people to remove from the squalor and temptations of the city and settle amid the wholesome helpful sights and sounds of country life. In a word, the people must be brought 'back to the land'.

Bournville Village was the result of George Cadbury having reached this conclusion; in fact it is reported he once remarked,

If I had not been brought into contact with the people in my Adult Class in Birmingham, and found from visiting the poor how difficult it was to lead a good life in a back street, I should probably never have built Bournville Village. (Ref. *The Birmingham News* supplement 28.10.1922.)

For the first 10 years after the founding of the Trust all net income was added to the Trust Fund and was available for further development of the Estate. After that sums were put each year to a 'Trustees' Special Expenditure' account, and devoted to such purposes as the endowment of a Lectureship in Town Planning at Birmingham University. Considerable sums were, and continue to be, spent on research into matters allied to housing and town planning. Although the first Trustees appointed were all members of the Cadbury family, provision was made for the later representation of the City of Birmingham, the University of Birmingham, and The Religious Society of Friends (Quakers), George Cadbury being a birthright member of the latter.

THE BOURNVILLE VILLAGE TRUST 'DEED OF FOUNDATION' 14th December 1900 gives details of the various parcels of land purchased between 1893 and 1900. Briefly they were as follows:

1893, March 4. 'Bournville Estate'.
Purchased from Trustees of JOSEPH STOCK, deceased.
All that irregularly-shaped piece of land in the Parishes of Kings Norton and Northfield, in the County of Worcestershire, containing 114a. 0r. 39p. bounded by Raddle Barn Lane, and in part by land belonging to the Guardians of the Poor of the Kings Norton Union; on the west in part by Oak Tree Lane, in part by Kings Norton Lane and in part by the Dell Cottage property; on the south in part by Bournville Lane and in other part by land belonging to Cadbury Bros. Limited, and on the east in part by land belonging to the Trustees of the Bournville Recreation Ground and in other part by land of the Midland Railway Company.

1894, October 5. Bournville Estate'.
Purchased from Trustees of JOSEPH STOCK, deceased.
A piece of land bounded on the north by Bournville Lane; on the south by Mary Vale Road; on the east by Linden Road, and on the west by Kings Norton Lane.

1895, June 25.
Purchased from E. S. Thackray.
Firstly. All that piece of land part of a piece of land called by the name of LONG PIECE, formerly known as SALLY BARN LEASOW . . . fronting in part to Oak Tree Lane, and in other parts to hereditaments belonging to EDWARD SPURR THACKRAY (and forming the grounds of DELL COTTAGE) and abutting backwards upon land now or late of JOSEPH STOCK and the said GEORGE CADBURY.

Secondly. All that piece of land . . . fronting to Oak Tree Lane aforesaid and situate on the opposite side of the said road to a certain cottage there, called YEW TREE COTTAGE, and which said piece of land runs from the hedge bounding the grounds of DELL COTTAGE aforesaid to a certain pump opposite YEW TREE COTTAGE aforesaid.

1895, September 28.
Purchased from Lewis Powell, 'The Beeches'.
All that triangular piece of land situate in and fronting to a certain road called Kings Norton Lane leading from Selly Oak to Kings Norton . . . abutting at the rear upon land of William and Wilson Moore.

1898, March 24.
Purchased from Frederick Elkington and others, 'Woodbrooke'.
All those pieces of land . . . fronting on the north-west side thereof in part to the main road there leading from Birmingham to Bromsgrove and in other part by land of the said George Cadbury and known as 'WOODBROOKE', and which said pieces or parcels of land contain together in the whole by estimation 83 acres or thereabouts, on some part whereof are erected certain messuages or dwelling-houses, two of which are known by the respective names of 'WOODBROOKE FARM' and 'YEW TREE FARM', and now or late in the respective occupations of PONSONBY LAWLEY and ROBERT KIRBY.

1899, September 27.
Purchased from the Trustees of John Abraham, deceased.
'Hay Green Estate'

All that and those messuages, farm house, cottages, closes, and parcels of land, farm and hereditaments situate in the Parish of Northfield in the County of Worcester, containing in whole 104a. 3r. 9p. or thereabouts.

Firstly. All that piece or parcel of land . . . formerly part of a larger piece of land called 'BLACK BEACH' containing 6a. 3r. 37p., fronting in part to Hay Green Road and in part to Kings Norton Lane.

Secondly. All that messuage or farm house with the outbuildings and the several closes or pieces of land known as 'THE HAY GREEN FARM' containing in the whole 13a. 0r. 9p. or thereabouts, bounded on the west by Cobs Lane, on the south by Hay Green Road, on the east in two lines by property of Miss Norcott and in the north by property of Lawrence Lawrence.

Thirdly. All those several closes . . . containing in the whole 24a. 0r. 38p., bounded on the north-west side thereof by Hay Green Road, on the west by Hole Farm Road, on the south-west by land formerly of the Trustees of the late John Abraham, but now of John Bentley and on the east by a new Road called WOODLANDS PARK ROAD.

Fourthly. All those parcels of land containing 14a. 3r. 37p. bounded on the west by a new Road called WOODLANDS PARK ROAD, on the north or north-north-west by Hay Green Road and on the east and south by land of William Moore and Wilson Moore.

Fifthly. All those several closes or parcels of land, in the whole 45a. 3r. 1p. bounded on the west by the said new road called WOODLANDS PARK ROAD, on the south in part by Northfield Road and in other part by land of the said John Bentley on the east by property of Arthur Adams and on the north-east by land of the said William Moore and Wilson Moore all which hereditaments formed part of certain lands containing 105a. 3r. 26p.

1899, September 27.

Purchased from Trustees of John Abraham, deceased, subject to Lease dated 19th December 1898.

All that piece of land . . . fronting to a road called Kings Norton Road leading from Kings Norton to Selly Oak, bounded on one side by land of Arthur Harry Griffin, and on the other side and at the back thereof by land formerly of the late John Abraham but now of the said George Cadbury.

1899, September 29.

Purchase from E. S. Thackray, 'The Dell'.

Firstly. All that piece or parcel of land being part of a piece or parcel of land called by the name of LONG PIECE, formerly known by the name of SALLY BARN LEASOW . . . fronting part to Oak Tree Lane and bounded on the north and east sides by land late of the Trustees of Joseph Stock but now of the said George Cadbury and on the south side also by other land of the said George Cadbury, whereon is erected a messuage or dwelling-house known by the name of 'DELL COTTAGE'.

Secondly. All that piece of land . . . fronting to Oak Tree Lane aforesaid and containing 241 square yards or thereabouts, whereon is erected a cottage.

1899, October 28) Purchased as to freehold interest from Joseph Ansell
1899, October 30) and as to leasehold interest from T. W. Halward.

All that piece of land fronting to a road called Kings Norton Road leading from Kings Norton to Selly Oak and Hay Green, bounded on one side by land now or late of Thomas Hemming, and at the back thereof by land of the said George Cadbury.

1900, May 24. Purchased from T. R. Bayliss
All that piece of land having a frontage to Cobs Lane, a frontage to Hay Green Road and a frontage to Road leading from Griffins Brook to Bristol road, and containing 10 acres and 10 perches.

1900, May 24. Purchased from Mrs Bayliss.
All that piece of land having a frontage to Cobs Lane and containing in the whole 2,171 square yards or thereabouts, whereon or on some part whereof are erected six messuages or dwelling houses fronting Cobs Lane.

1900, July 10. Exchanged with John Bentley. 'Hay Green'.
All that piece of land fronting to Woodlands Park Road and containing in front thereto 427 feet or thereabouts and containing in the whole 5,140 square yards or thereabouts.

A map accompanying the Deed of Foundation of the Bournville Trust, 1900, clearly shows the land belonging to Lawrence Lawrence encompassed Griffins Brook House, Woodbrooke Farm in addition to the area where we now have Dame Elizabeth Cadbury School, the Valley Parkway with the Yachting Pool.

Oakham Cottage and its land belonged to Mrs Elizabeth Norcott and Mrs Sarah Bardell. This later became Walker's Farm. The same area is roughly the lower part of Griffins Brook Lane, Hay Green Lane, Bournville Lane, taking in Frampton Close and Charfield Close.

Land belonging to William and Wilson Moore was referred to as Upper and Lower Rowheath. Covering a considerable area it stretched from the south side of lower Hay Green Lane taking in present day Cedar Road, part of Bournville Lane, Selly Oak Road to Northfield Road and westwards to Woodlands Park Road.

T. R. Bayliss owned land which extended from Hole Lane eastwards to Cob Lane. Mr Bayliss lived at 'Belmont', the site of present day 'Pocklington Place'.

The remaining landowner mentioned in the Deed of Foundation was J. Bentley Esq. and his land was sizeable, stretching from Bunbury Road to the western end of Hay Green Lane, and from Hole Lane eastwards to Woodlands Park Road.

Following the foundation of the Trust, more land was purchased during the first decade of the 20th century. Middle Park Farm was bought in 1903, the Middleton Hall Estate in 1905. Park Cottage Farm, later to be developed as the Weoley Hill Estate, was purchased in 1907.

In 1911 Rowheath Farm Estate was bought jointly by Bournville Trust and Cadbury Brothers.

The outbreak of the First World War in 1914 brought a halt to any further acquisition and it was to be another eight years before the next purchase of land was made. This time the site was in Hole Lane.

In 1929 The Trust bought Upper Shenley Fields Farm, followed by Yew Tree Farm. These areas were planned for development in the 1930's but only a handful of houses were built before the Second World War intervened and again building was curtailed. Once hostilities ceased building re-commenced and by the mid 1960's much of the area had been developed into a sizeable estate made up of houses, flats, maisonettes, a church, schools, doctor's surgery, and shopping centre.

While all this was going on, work was in progress at other points of The Bournville Estate. Woodbrooke Farm in Cob Lane was demolished in 1958 to make way for a block of offices for the Central Electricity Board and when that body relinquished the building it became the present day Bournville Lane West Midlands Police Station.

Middle Park Farm was also razed to the ground at about this time and its fields are now hidden by houses, flats, shops, a school and a college.

During the last quarter of the 20th century Trustees recognised the need for specialist housing for the elderly, single people, some with young children, the infirm and visually impaired, and various projects were undertaken.

A major development began in the late 70's at the Hole Farm and Priory area, adjacent to the Woodlands Orthopaedic Hospital, and it is made up solely of flats and houses. It was completed in 1980.

The proposal to build 33 houses and bungalows, including 14 for rent, on 'the horses' field' adjacent to the Valley Parkway in 1988 met with much hostility, as the area in question was considered to be the last bit of rural Bournville. I admit to being one of those who objected to the plans, and I still mourn the passing of the meadow with all the beauty it offered at the different seasons of the year. To me it was a wonderful back-drop to the Yachting Pool and I have often witnessed many folk throughout the years just sitting in a car, maybe recovering from an illness or maybe frail and infirm in their later years, quietly admiring the scene and taking up the feeling of tranquility it invoked. However, sentiment does not count for much these days, and people need homes; objections were over-ruled and development of Woodbrooke Meadow went ahead.

Recent years have seen the demolition of 'The Davids' in Hole Lane and the subsequent building of the mixed housing estate referred to as Wynds Point.

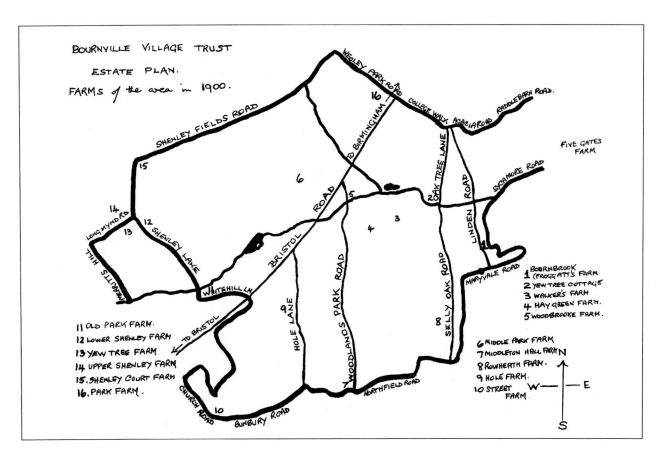

BOURNVILLE VILLAGE TRUST
ESTATE PLAN.
FARMS of the area in 1900.

WEOLEY PARK ROAD

SHENLEY FIELDS ROAD

COLLEGE WALK. ACACIA ROAD RADDLEBARN ROAD.

15

16

TO BIRMINGHAM

OAK TREE LANE

LINDEN ROAD

FIVE GATES FARM

SICAMORE ROAD

14

12 SHENLEY LANE

13

LONG MYND RD

MERRITTS HILL

6

BRISTOL ROAD

5

2

3

4

MARYVALE ROAD

WHITEHILL LN.

9

HOLE LANE

WOODLANDS PARK ROAD

SELLY OAK ROAD

8

1 BOURNBROOK
  (FROGGATT'S FARM
2 YEW TREE COTTAGE
3 WALKER'S FARM
4 HAY GREEN FARM.
5 WOODBROOKE FARM.

6 MIDDLE PARK FARM
7 MIDDLETON HALL FARM
8 ROWHEATH FARM.
9 HOLE FARM
10 STREET
   FARM

11 OLD PARK FARM.
12 LOWER SHENLEY FARM
13 YEW TREE FARM
14 UPPER SHENLEY FARM
15. SHENLEY COURT FARM
16. PARK FARM.

TO BRISTOL

CHURCH ROAD

10

BUNBURY ROAD

NORTHFIELD ROAD

N
W — E
S

61

Bournville Lane with Bournbrook Hall on the right.

BOURNBROOK HALL

Bournbrook Hall.

Bournbrook Hall, the main residence of the Bournbrook Hall Estate, is reported to have originally been the property of the Izon family before being bought by Thomas Stock, glass and lead merchant. Later a family named Martin were living there, and it was they who sold the Estate to George and Richard Cadbury in 1895. At that time it was considered to be over 100 years old. Iolo A. Williams in his book *The Firm of Cadbury 1831-1931* writes,

The purchase gave room, not only for future expansion of the Works themselves, but for the provision of more extensive recreation grounds.

Thus it was that in 1896 the 12 acres of grounds of Bournbrook Hall were landscaped into the Girls' Recreation Ground. More recently they have been recognised as part of Cadbury Schweppes' 'Bournville Club'. Perhaps I should stress at this point that this particular tract of land is not a part of the Bournville Estate; Cadbury the Firm and Bournville Village Trust have always functioned as two separate entities.

The Hall was demolished in 1907.

BOURNBROOK FARM

The old gate at the entrance to what was formerly Stock's Drive, now Linden Road opposite The Old Farm Hotel.

Situated at the corner of Linden Road and Bournville Lane, and sometimes referred to as Froggatt's Farm, parts of the original building can be seen at 'The Old Farm Hotel', tho' re-modelling was undertaken by W. Alexander Harvey, George Cadbury's architect at the beginning of the 20th century, when it became *Ye Olde Farm Inn.*

In the 1880's Mrs Sarah Froggatt and her step-son William were tenants of Bournbrook Farm. When Mrs Froggatt died in 1899, at the age of 84, she had been Bournville's oldest inhabitant for many years. In these days of alternative medicine, it is interesting to note she was renowned as a herbalist and curer of ailments and injuries. It is said that in the early days of the Cadbury Factory there was no Works Surgery, and so when workers injured themselves in the course of their work they invariably were sent to the farm to receive treatment.

In the 1880's one of the farm fields stretched from Bournville Lane north-wards to the Bourn brook which still flows in what is now Bournville Park. Normally used for the grazing of cattle, in 1883

Lily pond, Girls Recreation Grounds, looking to Bournville Village School in the distance.

The interior of the Old Farm Inn. *Early 1900's.*

Scouts' Night.

The Lofts, Bournville Lane, c.1952.

Bournville Cricket Club hired this field from William Froggatt and used it as their pitch until The Men's Recreation Ground was opened in 1896.

The Farm fields and buildings were home to a variety of animals, including chickens, cows and pigs and it is said William Froggatt would go to the factory kitchens once a week to collect two bucketsful of pig-swill which he would carry back to the farm by means of a yoke over his shoulder. (Half a century later I was to see a man with his lorry perform the same task!).

Prior to modern extensions being built during the late 50's and 60's there were quite extensive farm buildings to the rear of the Inn. Known as 'The Lofts', they for many years were utilised by various social groups including Junior Adult School, Camp-Fire Girls, Junior Young Friends (Quakers) and others.

During The Second World War, part of the premises were used by Friends' Relief Service as a depot for the collection, sorting, baling and distribution of clothing for refugees.

Now named *The Old Farm Hotel* the building is leased by The Bournville Village Trust to the present owner. The business is privately owned.

THE DELL COTTAGE and YEW TREE FARM *Oak Tree Lane*

Bentley's Worcestershire Directory, Northfield Section, dated 1841 includes Henry Elkington, gilder, as living at Dell Cottage. By the time of the 1851 census a William Bell was living there and by 1855 Billing's Listing for Northfield record Julius Partridge and E. S. Thackray as residents.

I think Dell Cottage must have been a little larger than its name implies, as I have in my possession a photograph which I am told shows The Staff of Elkington of Dell Cottage; four maids, a cook, coachman and gardener! George Cadbury bought the property from a Mr Elkington, and in 1909 it

became 'Fircroft' a working men's college.

During the 1940's the building was used to house young offenders. I presume the place was let to The Home Office at the time. Although it has been greatly extended and modernised in recent years 'The Dell' is still with us and is now the Head Office of Bournville Village Trust, 'The Estate Office'.

The Staff at Dell Cottage.

YEW TREE COTTAGE FARM

I am indebted to Mrs David Collier (neé Mary Roy) for the following account of life at Yew Tree Cottage farm during the 30's and 40's. Mary is a grand-daughter of Daniel Roy, who owned the bakery at Bournville.

> Our house was in two parts – the old section, in which there was a big beam running along the ceiling. Unfortunately, I think the old house had sunk slightly because when David (my husband to be) came to call he could walk under one end of the beam but would bang his head if he tried to cross the room near the fire-place!!

It was such fun living at Yew Tree Farm. As kids we could run up the stairs in the old house, passing the apple store on the way, go through my brother's bedroom, and by climbing three little steps and bending very low, we could open a little door and find ourselves at the top of the stairs in the newer part of the house. It was a wonderful place in which to play hide and seek.

The dairy was used as an Air Raid Warden's Station during the Second World War, and my father spent many hours on duty there with many local worthies.

My brother was away in Burma during the War, and the rest of us used to go to the

Rear view – Yew Tree Farm, Oak Tree Lane.

public Air Raid Shelter situated in the 'new road' as Woodbrooke Road was called for many years after it replaced the cinder-path which ran from Oak Tree Lane to Bristol Road. Occasionally, when air raids continued for several hours, my father would appear with mother's best cups, one in each pocket, and a flask of hot cocoa for everyone.

I think I must have told about our cat who used to follow daddy everywhere. When a land-mine dropped very nearby, the cat was blown spread-eagled into the hedge whilst daddy was hanging on to a lamp-post. We didn't see the cat for three days, but, eventually, his love for daddy overcame his fear of any land-mine!!

One thing I can always remember as a child was waking (in the summer months) to the sound of horses' hooves as the draymen walked their horses from the field (now Meadow rise), to the Bakery on The Green to start their day's work. During the winter months the horses were housed in our stables.

My cousins and I used to have such fun as children sitting on the bakery carts and pretending we were cowboys! Our pleasures were never expensive – there wasn't much money – but we had such fun.

Yew Tree Cottage.

Another person who remembers what life was like during the 20's and 30's is Mrs Rita Wallace (neé Brough). She lived opposite Yew Tree Farm, in fact she still lives in the same house. I am grateful to her for allowing me to quote the following.

Yachting Pool with 'the horses' field' in the background.

I was born at a house in Oak Tree Lane. My parents had married at Harborne church and settled in Bournville. We lived on what was then the edge of the village and we looked out on to field upon field. We were virtually in the country.

Opposite our home was Yew Tree Farm where I remember going to get milk and cream, etc. The dairy was down three steps and was always very cold. The milk was stored in churns with different measures hanging round the edge. They were all made of copper. In later years it ceased to be a farm but the stables continued to house the horses from Roy's bakery each winter. *[I can remember the time when some of the outbuildings were used by Harry Ward, a local electrician, and one of the*

72

YEW-TREE COTTAGE AND ENTRANCE TO WOODBROOKE PATHWAY · 1934

Yew Tree Cottage at corner of Woodbrooke Road and Oak Tree Lane.

73

tasks I had to do, as a child, was to take the accumulator from the radio to be charged.] Just up the road was the cinder-path – a footpath cutting through the fields to the Bristol Road, and later used as a way to get to the tramway when the route was extended to the Lickey Hills. At the end of the path was Lucas's farm where they kept a dairy herd. This was Woodbrooke Farm.

We children played in the fields, which were always full of long meadow-grass, and we

Mrs May Roy in the garden of Yew Tree Cottage.
Note the dovecot and farm buildings

paddled in the brook which meandered through them. There was also a large muddy pond which was surrounded by bullrushes and full of newts and frogs. One or other of us invariably fell in, much to the annoyance of our parents. To the south of the farm there was a few cottages dotted about. On the other side of the lane there was a very imposing 'Gatehouse' which had once been the entrance to a large residence, Griffins Brook House. Long since demolished, its remains surrounded by tall trees and overgrowth, led to us believing the place was haunted and we always ran past!

Down the road was Bournville Park – our playground. In the park was the shop – just a shed whose side opened up to form a counter. It was owned by a Mr and Mrs Summers who lived in Thorn Road. They sold all the sweets of the time; kalisuckers, liquorice sticks, bulls-eyes, gob-stoppers (they changed colour as you sucked them), nougat, liquorice boot-laces, aniseed balls and lovely home-made custardy ice-cream. Most things only cost a halfpenny or penny.

The park-keeper was always around ('parky' as we called him). We were always a little frightened of him, tho' I can't think why as we did very little in the way of damage. In those days the park was surrounded by spiked railings and had several gateway entrances. It was 'parky's' job to ring a hand-bell at dusk before clearing the park and locking the gates. Those were the days when we played hide-and-seek, tig, tops and whips, bowls, skipping ropes, five stones and marbles. (The gates and railings were removed during the Second World War and sent off to be melted down to help the 'war effort'.)

The whole area was a wonderful habitat for birds and wild animals. Blackbirds, thrushes, robins, blue-tits, as well as woodpeckers, water-wagtails, the occasional kingfisher, and at night we would hear owls. There were doves and bats living in the dovecot at Yew Tree Farm.

There was a rabbit warren at the top of the horses' field and our neighbour's cat would sometimes bring a young live one home and our neighbour would duly take it back.

We went fishing in the brooks, trying to catch stickle-backs. On one such occasion we saw a crayfish and sometimes we would hear a splash as a water vole darted about.

The fields were full of wild flowers, some of them quite rare and sadly we no longer see them in the area today.

Woodbrooke Farm

BOURNVILLE COUNCIL YEAR BOOK for 1919 gives Ponsonby and Emma Lawley as residents of Woodbrooke Farm. By 1929 the name W. Lucas appears. Situated in Cob Lane, near the junction with Bristol Road, it was, as I have already stated, a dairy farm.

Elizabeth M. Cadbury when serving as a Bournville Trustee in 1935 wrote the following minute after visiting Woodbrook Farm.

> Here we met Mr C. A. Lucas who showed us the old stable which has been converted into a sterilising room with a cold store in one corner. We did the floor and ceiling for him, and his son installed all the steam and water fittings himself. We also saw an old well which has been opened up; it is hoped to fix a pump and use this supply of cold water for cooling the milk.

Woodbrooke Farm was demolished in 1958 and its fields have all but vanished, making way for the offices and car park of Bournville Lane, West Midlands Police Force. I say all but vanished, because one area of greenery, complete with its meandering brook, still survives and gives pleasure to those who walk its pathways. Michael Harrison, in his book *BOURNVILLE 'Model Village to Garden Suburb'* writes;

> There were times when the Trustees had to balance the amenity value of the landscape against the commercial value of certain plots of land. The land opposite the South Birmingham Technical College on Bristol Road was a case in point. The plots had originally been zoned for commercial development, but Herbert Manzoni, the City Engineer and Surveyor, later expressed the view that the plots should instead be kept as open spaces. By the spring of 1960 the building for Wagon Repairs and the Central Electricity Board [*now the W. M. Police Station*] at the end of Bournville Lane were both nearing completion. The Trust

Woodbrooke Farmhouse.

The Drive, Woodbrooke Farm.

Turkeys, Woodbrooke Farm.

The Yard, Woodbrooke Farm.

Farm Cottages.

were anxious to develop two adjacent plots. If those sites were left undeveloped this would, of course, involve considerable financial loss to the Trust. They argued that these commercial sites could be successfully landscaped, just as the two buildings nearing completion and the nearby College and schools had been.

To help them try to solve the issue the Trust called in G. A. Jellicoe, the well-known landscape architect. He was asked 'to advise them upon the most agreeable development, having in mind both the economic and the landscape interests'. Although he felt that the site could be developed in an informal and agreeable way for commercial uses, Jellicoe came down in favour of retaining the open landscape which he considered a potentially important part of this unusually distinguished highway approach to Birmingham, he concluded:

> I have no hesitation in recommending . . . that this land should remain as existing, provided it is opened up and becomes part of the scenery of the main road. I would add that it seems to me that this romantic view of Bournville, in contrast to the enjoyable but fleeting glimpse along Bournville Lane, would give the motorist a very happy awareness of a project that was first of its kind in England.

Adjacent to Woodbrooke Farm were two semi-detached cottages. Still in situ today, they are said to be the oldest inhabited dwellings on the Bournville Estate. They are believed to have been built in the late 17th century and originally provided homes for Woodbrooke farm-workers. Rumour has it the exposed beams were originally ship's timbers. What tales these cottages could tell, built as they are on Cob Lane which is thought to have once been a section of the Highway used by the Birmingham to Bristol Stage-coach!

Middle Park Farm

THE EARLIEST RECORD I have found relating to Middle Park Farm is the census for 1851 which tells us it was in the Shendley Yield and covered an area of 110 acres. A William Smout and his family were living there at the time.

Mr Oscar Hopkins of Northfield has kindly allowed me to see a copy of his Family Tree. It tells us that a Marshall Frederick Johnson, born at Oldbury in 1824, married a Sophia Upton from Tamworth in 1856. They lived for a time at Rowley Regis, where they had a Brick-Yard, but later moved to Middle Park Farm, Selly Oak, which was bought to keep horses for Selly Oak and Metchley brick-yard's haulage work. Their first son, Walter, also farmed Middle Park. His sister, Polly, was Oscar Hopkins's mother. I am grateful to Mr Hopkins for giving me permission to use this information.

In 1888 the farm was being worked by a Mr Lucas.

The Bournville Village Council Year Book for 1928 devotes a whole page to advertise the farm. It reads;

THE BEST MILK

1888   1928

Forty Years

Hygienic Dairying

America Drinks One Pint of Milk per Head per Day

Other Countries More

WAKE UP ENGLAND

Drink more Fresh Milk

You can get the Best Fresh Milk

'Nature's Best and Most Perfect Food'

LUCAS

Middle Park Farm

Bristol Road, Selly Oak

and

Woodbrooke Farm

Cob Lane, Bournville.

Cowsheds Lighted by Electricity

The Cream on our Bottled Milk is THE BEST for

Infants and Invalids!

In 1935 Bournville Village Trustees reported on the Farm buildings as follows:

> We do not keep the buildings up very well now as they will have to come down before very long on account of building development.

In fact the Second World War intervened, which led, yet again, to the suspension of building development and it wasn't until 1958 that the demolition of Middle Park Farm took place. As a result we now have Bournville College of Further Education, flats, shops, a school and a sizeable housing estate, in addition to The Manor Park Estate of flats. The latter, not a part of The Bournville Estate, is owned by The City of Birmingham.

The accompanying photographs give us a pictorial glimpse of Middle Park Farm and some of its out-buildings, together with machinery used during the early part of the 20th century and some of the farm animals. Can you believe cows were led across Bristol Road each day as recently as 1958?

Mowing and Tedding with Middle Park Farmhouse in the background.

Out-buildings, Middle Park Farm.

Middle Park Farmland.

Tedding.

85

Threshing.

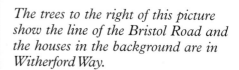

The trees to the right of this picture show the line of the Bristol Road and the houses in the background are in Witherford Way.

Ploughing. The row of houses on the left of this picture are in Middle Park Road. The white house is in Swarthmore Road.

The house in the top right-hand corner is no. 54 Green Meadow Road.

Farmland with Bryony House,
Bryony Road, just behind the Oak Tree
– looking towards Rowheath.

The same area two years later.

Harvest-time. Bournville School, Griffins Brook Lane, in the background.

Cows being driven across Bristol Road with houses of Middle Park Road in the background.

89

Hay Green Farm and Walker's Farm

THERE WERE TWO FARMS situated in Hay Green Lane, Hay Green, sometimes referred to as Sheward's farm and Walker's Farm, believed at one time to be called Oakham Cottage.

Records of Hay Green Farm and its occupants go back to around 1540 in the Northfield Parish Register according to G. Letitia Hayes in her book Old Hay Green Lane. She tells us that behind the farm there were cowsheds, a dairy, pigsties with orchards and fields beyond. Stables were built around the farm-yard, as were sheds to house the various carts and farm implements. There was a big barn where the children were allowed to play.

According to The Northfield Societies occasional paper no. 4 *Manors and Vestry in Northfield*,

> A certain George Attwood deceased who had purchased two houses and lands in Hay Field held by the service of a Red Rose upon the Feast of St Michael the Baptist and a peppercorn. By his will George Attwood hath devised (bequeathed) one of the said messuages situate at Hay Green and about 124 acres (part of the estate later occupied by Mr Thomas Willetts) unto Mr James Attwood and the other messuage called Middleton Hall about 181 acres unto Matthias Attwood.

The Trade directories for 1841 record a Thomas Harrison as being the occupant of Hay Green at that time.

For many years Hay Green Farm was farmed by a family named Sheward and as a result it became known as Sheward's Farm. Mrs Betty Sheward of Bournville recalls her late husband telling her that, as a boy, he and sometimes a friend as well, would play truant from school and hide in the barns. Mrs Sheward goes on to say,

Hay Green Farm.

Hay Green Farm in a derelict state.

91

Hay Green Farm 1897 from a painting by J. H. Hipsley.

Hay Green Lane with Hay Green Farm on the left. The Lane on the right later became Mulberry Road.

I know sometimes my mother-in-law used to help deliver the milk and used to see Laurence Cadbury on horseback at times. I believe the farm came down in 1927/28 to build houses there. When no. 1 Old Barn Road was built Harry and Walter Sheward lived there, sons of the farmer 'grand-dad Sheward'.

Hay-making, Walker's Farm.

The houses Mrs Sheward refers to are those in the present day Old Barn Road, Griffins Brook Lane, Hay Green Lane area.

Again I turn to a book by G. Letitia Haynes, *A New Home in a Model Village* and I am grateful to her executors for allowing me to quote her picturesque account of Hay Green Lane in the twenties.

Hay Green Lane in those days was known as 'the dark lane', it was little more than a narrow, muddy, rutted cart-track, with high, overgrown banks on each side, tunnelled over with ancient trees, very like Constable's painting *The Cornfield*.

The banks were topped with hedgerows through which dog-roses scrambled, fragrant in the dew of summer mornings, or in their seasons, rich with a harvest of elderberries, black-berries, hazel nuts, and wild strawberries. Birds of innumerable species nested high and low along its length, and in spring-time their dawn chorus poured out loud and clear, giving a sense of inner joy and lasting values, the like of which has vanished completely from the English countryside. Little Gallows Brook chattered and skipped merrily along one side, making such a nuisance of itself in wet weather, when it overflowed its banks and flooded the lane, making it all but impassable. At the end of the lane it flowed past a few small cottages, each of which had a little bridge over the stream leading into the front garden.

As I have already said, there were two farms in close proximity to each other and from maps it is clear that one was much bigger than the other. Again I am able to quote Miss Haynes.

Hay Green Farm was the more easy-going of the two, they never minded children picking wind-fall fruit in the orchard; they let them mix the swill and feed for the pigs; they let them rattle the corn tin to summon the many fowls running at will in the farm-yard, adjacent out-buildings and fields, and then scatter the contents to the expectant flock; they let them collect the warm, newly-laid eggs from the straw-lined nesting boxes when the hen's triumphant cackle announced her achievement, or gave them a basket to hunt eggs around the hedgerows or out-houses where hens had laid astray; they let them feed apples or carrots or anything else they had brought or could find, to the big, gentle cart-horses. Nobody seemed to notice when children turned the handle of the chaffing machine which could have cut off their hands; nobody saw any danger and no accident happened.

Best of all was the big barn where a large old sofa had been suspended with ropes from one of the big beams. Children romped on it unceasingly, the ride ending with a good deep tumble in the hay.

Walker's Farm was owned by 'granny Walker' a vigorous old lady in her nineties, who, after the death of her husband many years before, had managed and worked the farm herself, as her eldest son had emigrated to Canada. She had had a number of children, but they all married and left her, with the exception of one daughter who was still with her at the farm. Her second son's wife had died, leaving a growing-up family, including two young children. She took in the lot, ruling them firmly but with a lot of shrewd wisdom. She kept a sharp eye on all the children who made their way up to the farm and showed them clearly just what was, and was not allowed, but indeed it was rare for a child to do much wanton damage or seriously to annoy the farm folks.

I have been fortunate enough to find a relative of the afore-mentioned 'granny Walker'. She is Mrs Jillian Stokes of Rednal, Birmingham, and she told me that her mother, Ann (Nancy) Walker, was brought up from the age of 11 months by Sara and Ellen Walker, her grandmother and aunt respectively, at Oakham Cottage. She sometimes talked about life at the farm. They kept chickens, ducks, pigs and at least one cow. She remembered the cow in particular as it had tossed her when she was a little girl! Ann Walker also recalled having to walk, as a child, up Oak Tree Lane to Selly Oak to fetch animal feed before going to school. Mrs Stokes goes on to say how happy her mother was when she talked about the farm; sleeping in a four-poster bed and drawing the curtains when the weather was cold; listening to the crystal radio set.

The family remained at Oakham until the death of 'granny Walker'. Soon afterwards the farm was demolished to make way for further development of Hay Green Lane / Bournville Lane. George Cadbury had always insisted 'the old lady' would not be moved from her home while she was alive!

Haymaking was a happy time and Mrs Stokes has kindly loaned me a treasured family photograph which shows her mother, father and sister sitting on the cart. Unfortunately I have been unable to find a photograph or picture of Oakham Cottage.

Hole Farm

A MEDIUM-SIZED FARM of around 64 acres, owned by a John Pope in 1838 and occupied at that time by a Benjamin Cutler. From Trade Directories dated 1841 we read that John Green was the occupying farmer. The census for 1851 records the farm as being in the Hay-with-Middleton Yield and Joseph Meredith, varnish maker, being the occupier.

In 1899 Hole Farm, together with a great deal of neighbouring land, was sold as Lots at the sale of a Freehold, Residential and Building Estate belonging to the Estate of the late John Abraham Esq.

I am indebted to Mr Ivor Cooke, of Hole Lane, Bournville, for allowing me to quote from correspondence he wrote in reply to my request for information about Hole Farm.

> My grandparents moved to Hole Farm in 1892, and their unmarried daughter, Miss Dorothy Guest Garland, died there in 1964. They were not farmers! But farming was carried on by employees; a small dairy herd; a milk round; pigs; poultry; and latterly a minimal amount of horticulture.
>
> I was born at the Davids Cottage in 1920, where we lived until 1925, in which year Laurence Cadbury bought 'The Davids' and required the cottage for one of his staff. My present home [*a few yards from Hole Farm*] was built by my grandparents on their land in 1905. I lived here as a child from 1927 to 1932; and again from 1955.
>
> The farm and land were originally rented from John Abraham who lived, and operated as major landowner from 'The Woodlands', Bristol Road. When he died my family bought the farm and land, out-bidding the Cadburys at the auction of the Estate.

I have a George III penny in an old envelope on which is written in my aunt's handwriting, 'This penny was found embedded in the wall at the bottom of Hole Farm Garden when it was broken down by the great flood of 1927.'

Between the Farmhouse and the brook was a walled garden. One wall (still standing) lay between the orchard and the garden. One wall was alongside Hole Lane, the house was on the south-side, and the fourth boundary was the brook. The storm water flooded the garden and

The junction of Heath Road South and Hole Farm Road, originally Hole Farm land.

the wall fell into the brook. I remember the storm. (I was aged seven.)

The penny is dated 1799 and I think that is probably the date that the farm and the walls were built, though almost certainly a farm was there before, probably very much older, since

Hole Farm Fields.

Hole Lane is an ancient thoroughfare. The farm is Georgian, though the front was Victorianised, and the windows are very much 19th century.

Bournville Village Trust acquired the Hole Farm Estate from the executors of Miss Dorothy Guest Garland in 1954, and from 1958 their Chief Architect of the time, Selby Clewer, and his wife and family lived in the farmhouse. One daughter still lives there today. Selby Clewer has kindly written the following account for me.

My personal memories of Hole Farm go back to 1958. There were some nine acres of pasture which for some years had been let for grazing. The Garland family had been in residence for several generations. Miss Garland seems to have been a person of some character. A great tennis player in her younger years – there were two courts still at the rear of the farmhouse when we went there in 1958 – and a lover of the theatre – Marie Lloyd is reputed to have stayed with her when she was touring in Birmingham.

The house seems to have been built in the latter half of the 18th century and to have had a good 'going over' in late Victorian times when the steeply pitched dormer windows were put in, hall tiles laid and the heavy plaster cornice in the two front rooms applied.

The staircase and most of the internal doors are from the 18th-century work but the windows are Victorian and possibly not in the same places as the original ones. There is still a very deep chimney breast in the left-hand front room which might have been the original kitchen – maybe even from an earlier building on the same site.

When we took over there was no mains water, no electricity and only one gas point (on the second floor where Miss Garland lived), and a gas-light point in the kitchen downstairs. Water was from a well – still existing in the back yard, and to a tap over a large brick sink in the scullery from a semi-rotary pump connected to an underground cistern fed from roof water which was also collected in an open-air tank formed in a roof valley which fed a single

W.C. on the first floor. The tank leaked and the whole of that part of the house was infested with dry-rot.

Miss Garland did not approve of new-fangled conveniences it seems! She had a maid, Rose, who asked us if we could take on the garden 'boy' who had been with them since the 'war' – the 1914 one it transpired.

There were two staircases and the back part of the house had been built at a later date than the other and was not connected to it except at ground-floor level.

The out-buildings in 1955 consisted of the Coach House which still exists with a stable for two horses at the rear and behind that a tack room and pigsties with two lofts over and a lean-to greenhouse at the back of that. On the other side of the stable-yard was a cart-shed with a loft over which was used by the local scouts of which Mr Ivor Cooke, Miss Garland's nephew, was leader.

On the north side of the yard at the back of the farmhouse itself was a short range containing a brewhouse and coalhouse backing on to the wall of the orchard which occupied the present open space to the north which goes down to the stream. The eastern wall was right on the present kerb-line.

The trees were mainly damson and dead or dying; on the west side of the orchard under the yew tree was a derelict three-hole earth closet.

Overlooking the lower tennis court and with its back to the stream was the remains of a wooden summer-house, but there was no other building on the agricultural land. This extended from The Davids in the north, the convent in the west to the backs of the houses on the south-side of Heath Road South.

The following appeared in *The Carillon,* spring 1989.

Close to Hole Lane lies Garland Way Pool which is being re-landscaped. Prior to the Hole Farm development in the mid 1960's, there was a pool here which was called 'Garland's Pool' after the Garland family who lived at Hole Farm. It was originally dug to provide water for cattle and was topped up by the local brook. However, part of the pool encroached on land owned by Mr Richard Bayliss of 'BELMONT' and in the olden days the boundary was marked by a line of fence-posts in the water. The footpath alongside the pool dates from the late 1930's.

Rowheath Farm

SITUATED at the southern end of Selly Oak Road, near the junction with Northfield Road, Rowheath, in the Haye-with-Middleton Yield was a sizeable farm of 128 acres. In 1838 it was owned by a John Moore and occupied and worked by a Samuel Gregg.

By 1900, the plan accompanying The Bournville Trust Deed of Foundation marks the land as belonging to William and Wilson Moore.

The Rowheath Farm Estate was bought jointly by Cadbury Brothers and Bournville Village Trust in 1911. Some of the original farm buildings can still be seen today. Now referred to as 'The Old Beams' the building in question is a timber-framed structure which originally had wattle and daub in the 1800's. Whenever the present day building is put on the market, the sales brochure mentions the fact that the barn-doors have been replaced with high, tall windows and as a result a lovely natural light fills the building. Exposed beams are visible in most of the rooms.

In addition to the barn a further timber-framed building of the same period can be found nearby. Known as 'The Coach-house', it may well have once been the farm dairy.

In *A Bournville Assortment* I quote the following from The Bournville Council Year Book dated 1925.

> Some 10 years ago land amounting to about 70 acres was purchased to provide additional playing grounds for Bournville (Cadbury) employees.

> Owing to the war, the development of the grounds was postponed, but with the formation of the Works Departmental Games Association, the greatly increased demand for facilities led to the rapid development of the grounds. As time went on, further fields were converted into

playing areas and as the whole of the grounds became more and more developed, plans were prepared for the laying out of a Garden Club, a scheme which would absorb nine acres out of the total 70 acres of land. The leading features of the Garden Club are the Central Pavilion, a large lawn and a model lake. Spaces have been reserved for the playing of clock-golf, croquet, etc. There are two open-air stages, one on either side of the extreme end of the lawn. The Lawn has been largely used for dancing, while the provision of the model lake has resulted in the formation of a Model Yacht Club. The Central Pavilion is a prominent land-mark, being situated on high ground. French windows open out from the front of the Pavilion on to a terrace which overlooks the lawn below.

During the Second World War, much of the playing field area was handed over for the cultivation of cereal crops, whilst the Pavilion and gardens were used as a venue for public social gatherings, such as Ballroom dances, Olde-Tyme dances, Choral and Orchestral concerts.

In recent years 65 acres of land at

Rowheath in the 1920's – looking north.

Rowheath have been developed resulting in the provision of both privately owned dwellings and housing schemes for the elderly. This particular scheme was planned with energy conservation in mind and a Demonstration House drew much national and international interest at an Open Day in 1985. Little wonder the area is now referred to as 'The Solar Village'.

Rowheath in the 1930's with Rowheath farmland in the background.

Middleton Hall Farm

READERS WILL REALISE BY NOW, how much I have been able to quote from the 20 or so occasional papers that have been published over the years by the 'Northfield Society' (originally referred to as 'The Northfield Conservation Group'), and I thank them, particularly Mrs Margaret J. Lane, for allowing me to use items of narrative. In her booklet, entitled *Life on a Farm in Northfield 1789*, Mrs Lane writes;

> Farming did not begin very early in Northfield; people chose areas where the soil was easier to work, but in Domesday Book 1086, we find that farmers had begun to work the clay soil here. The land was first farmed in strips without hedges and the animals grazed on Common land; that is land held by all the village. This meant that diseases spread easily. So farmers wanted to put all their strips together to make bigger fields. Each owner had to pay for enclosing his land and people who could not pay lost their land. In Northfield there was only gradual enclosure and much common grazing was left until the 19th century. Several compact farms were formed and one of these was Middleton Hall Farm.

> We know quite a lot about Middleton Hall Farm because in 1789 it was farmed by William Henshaw who kept a note book diary. This book is now in the Birmingham Reference Library.

> Middleton Hall Farm was a timber-framed building thought to have been built in the 16th century. It stood where Redmead Close is now. In Victorian times it was coated with bricks to make a fashionable house. It was pulled down in 1953 and all that remains is a converted cottage. The fields lay both sides of Burnbury Road.

In 1789 it was a prosperous farm with enough home-grown produce for most of their needs and a surplus of grain and cheese to sell as well as sheep and cattle that would have been sold to the local butcher.

Beside her work looking after the children and supervising the cooking and serving of meals, a farmer's wife was expected to do many other things. She would look after the hens, and the money she received from the sale of eggs was usually considered to be her 'pocket-money'. The fowl would run freely around the farmyard and in the nearby fields. They would have to be fed scattered corn or dried peas twice a day. At night they would be shut up in a hen-house to protect them from foxes.

When I contacted Mrs Lane to seek permission to use the above, she stressed she had written the booklet with children in mind. I have used only a little of her narrative here, but would fully recommend the booklet, together with its descriptive illustrations by Veronica McDermot, to children of all ages.

Other records of Middle Hall Farm tell us its 181 acres were bequeathed by George Attwood's will to Mathias Attwood in 1813.

By 1838 the farm had become the property of George Attwood (was he a son of Mathias Attwood, I wonder?) and the occupier was Robert Thornley.

Records dated 1851 tell us Middleton Hall Farm was in the sub-manor of Haye-and-Middleton, had its manor house at Middleton Hall, meadow at Longmeadow, and waste at Row Heath. A windmill is said to have stood near Middleton Hall at one time.

The map which accompanies the Bournville Village Trust Deed of Foundation dated 14th December 1900 shows Middleton Hall Farm and its land as belonging to J. Bentley.

Street Farm

S TREET FARM, covering an area of 105 acres, was reported to be one of the larger farms in the Northfield parish in 1838 and was owned by Robert Fenwick, Trustee to the Rev. John Thomas Fenwick.

The occasional paper no. 8 published by The Northfield Conservation Group is entitled *Northfield in the Old Trade Directories*. Its cover is a copy of Bentley's Worcestershire Directory for 1841 and records a Charles Robinson living at Street Farm.

Ethel Adair Impey, in her book *Northfield in 1851*, states that at that time Street Farm was occupied by Miss Wilson, Billy Field and a Mr Blunn.

By the middle of the 20th century the farm had fallen into decay. Mr Selby Clewer writes;

> The farmstead itself was largely ruinous and covered with ivy, but it had 17th-century features. It was situated in Church Road, Northfield, where the Y.M.C.A. building and private bungalows now are at the end of Heath Road South. This road was intended to form part of a through route from Great Stone Road to Pershore Road, at Stirchley, via Heath Road and Maryvale Road, but the island planned at the junction with Church Road was never constructed, much to the relief of Heath Road residents!

I am grateful to Sarah Foden, Information Manager, Information and Library Service, Cadbury Limited, for allowing me to quote the following 'Story of Street Farm' from the Bournville Works Magazine dated December 1958.

> Readers who live in the Northfield area, and indeed many others, must have noticed, with some regret, that the ivy-covered house, known as Street Farm, opposite the road leading off

to 'The Great Stone Inn' and St Laurence's Church, has been demolished. As can be seen from the photograph (taken after the ivy had been removed) it was a well-proportioned house. The main building dated from about 1700. The ground floor addition, which can be seen on the right, was obviously made much later, certainly less than 100 years ago. This extra 'wing' included a sitting-room large enough to take a billiard table, and also a bedroom and small kitchen.

According to Mr William Field, better known locally as 'Billy Field', who was a tenant from early in this century until 1936, this addition was made about 1850 by the owner, who lived at Edgbaston and used to drive out to Northfield, then in the country, for the excellent shooting available at Street Farm. He is reputed to have reared pheasants, and there was a good stock of wild partridges and hares. At that time the farm fields stretched down to the Convent [*Maryland Drive*] and Hole Lane. The sporting owner was probably Lt.-Col. James Miller, who sold the farm in 1880 to Stephen Barker, from whose widow, Mrs Beatrice Dumurgue Barker, George Cadbury purchased the property in 1895.

The condition of the interior of the farm-house was so poor that it was not a practicable proposition to save it, and indeed there could have been no question of preservation, because Heath Road South will join Church Road at this point. The old kitchen range was an interesting period piece, dating to the days when cast iron was a favourite material for builders and engineers. The present-day housewife would look askance at it, however. It must have involved an enormous amount of work in cleaning and stoking, and have consumed prodigious amounts of fuel. Another interesting feature of the inside of Street Farm was the old doors, which were built from local elm.

The Bournville Works Magazine published in September 1964 carries an article which tells us the Birmingham Y.M.C.A. at Bunbury Road, Northfield, has been built on a site previously occupied by Street Farm, the main building of which dates from 1700. At one time the farm stood in rural solitude and was well known for the partridge, pheasant and hare which provided particularly good shooting'.

Street Farm – now demolished.

Whitehill or Old Park Farm

IN 1820 DANIEL LEDSAM, Lord of Weoley Manor, offered several farms for sale including WHITEHILL (Old Park). The farmer at that time was a William Willet.

Occasional paper no. 16 issued by the Northfield Society in 1984, carries a list of medium sized farms in Northfield parish in 1838 and Whitehill is mentioned. Extending to 59 acres 0 rods and 9 poles, it was owned and occupied by John Allen.

The Ordnance Survey map dated 1884 shows the farm situated at the western end of White Hill Lane, at the junction with Shenley Lane.

The farmland has been taken up by housing mainly, although some green fields and hedgerows can still be seen in the vicinity of Shenley Lane Community Association and Sports Centre. One building remains; now named 'Old Park Cottage', I am told it is the original farmhouse.

I am indebted to Bournville Village Trustees for allowing me to quote the following extract from a report submitted to Trustees in August 1935. It is signed by Elizabeth M. Cadbury.

I should like to advise the Trustees that I visited the farm

Old Park Cottage – Whitehill Lane.

properties on 31st July accompanied by R. G. Salter (Land agent) and L. P. Appleton (Secretary and Manager) and F. R. Barlow (Assistant Secretary).

UPPER SHENLEY FARM

We met Mr Powell, the energetic young tenant. He told us he was going in largely for pig production and was now keeping 210 pigs. He hopes to erect a piggery for another 60. We inspected a piggery where four litters are kept in indoor sties under the Danish system. I was much interested to find that Mr Powell had adopted the Danish method of keeping pigs – I visited the Agricultural School when I was last in Denmark. We also looked at two good indoor sties which have been formed by an alteration in the barn.

The tenant produces Grade A Milk. The small cow-shed is very low but the large cow-shed, enlarged a few years ago, is a very good shed.

I noted that the end of the large barn had to be re-built this year and that the old wagon-shed has been re-roofed and repaired.

SHENLEY COURT FARM

This small farm is worked in conjunction with Upper Shenley Farm.

Mrs Sylvia Latham, daughter of Norman and Bessie Powell, one time farmers of Shenley Court and Shenley Hill Farms, has kindly contributed her personal memories of life on the farms.

Tom Powell took over the tenancy of Shenley Hill Farm in 1927/28 when the previous tenant, Mr Randall, retired to a house on the opposite side of Shenley Hill.

Upper Shenley Farmhouse.

Upper Shenley Farmyard.

Crossing the yard, Upper Shenley.

113

Potato Harvest – Upper Shenley.

*Land Army Girl – 2nd World War –
Upper Shenley.*

Potatoes ready for market.

Making a hay-rick.

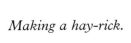

115

Upper Shenley, looking towards the Weoley Castle Estate.

Upper Shenley, looking towards Northfield.

116

Until Tom and his wife Emily were able to move into Shenley Hill, my parents, Norman and Bessie Powell, became farm managers for them and occupied the premises. Eventually Tom and Emily moved in and both families lived together for a time until, in 1931, my parents moved to Shenley Court Farm and farmed there until 1938.

In 1938 Tom Powell bought a farm at Stoke Prior, Bromsgrove and Norman Powell and his family moved to

This shows farmland of Shenley Court Farm. In fact it is Shenley Fields Road at the junction of Gorse Close.

Shenley Hill Farm. At the time my granny, together with my aunt and uncle, Jessie and Frank Powell (sister and brother), moved from Shropshire to Shenley Court Farm. My granny died in 1942 and uncle Frank died in 1946. Aunty Jessie continued farming, with the help of another brother, Reg. He and his family had moved to Birmingham in the early 30's to work for Tom Powell and then for Frank and Jessie. Reg was responsible for the milk-retailing side of the farm. He lived in Shenley Fields Road.

Both farms were mixed farming, with cows, pigs and arable, and working horses. The crops grown were wheat, barley, oats, with potatoes and a few greens, and mangolds for animal feed. There was a small amount of land that was set aside for animal grazing.

When tractors became common-place we still kept a shire horse for drawing carts, etc. My father's main interest was pedigree pigs and he bred 'large whites'. We kept a few free-range hens, mainly for domestic use, and I kept geese.

On both farms they pasteurised, bottled and retailed milk to the local estate – Weoley Castle – until the late forties when that part of the business was sold to a larger concern.

Shenley Hill Farm had two cottages attached and these were occupied by farm workers and their families.

Shenley Court had a cottage which was separate from the farmhouse. During the Second World War there was a searchlight, a large gun, and barrage balloon station situated on Shenley Hill land. The Fire Brigade used the farmhouse as a fire-watching post and the Home Guard also occupied part of the building all through the war. Dad and the farm workers were all members of the Home Guard. Both farms were owned by Bournville Village Trust. In approximately 1952 Shenley Court land ceased to be used for farming and was built on.

Shenley Hill was sold to the City of Birmingham Education Committee in 1954 and Norman and Bessie Powell moved to 108 Green Meadow Road. The farmland was used to house Shenley Court Comprehensive School, opened in 1963.

The Powell family all came from the Whixall, Coton and Wem area of Shropshire.

(Land on the southern side of Shenley Hill now belongs to Birmingham City Council and has been spared development thus far. Long may it retain its rural features.)

Yew Tree Farm

WHEN I FIRST BEGAN my research into the farmsteads of the Bournville Estate area, I knew very little about Yew Tree Farm, in fact for some time I had an idea it and Lower Shenley Farm were one and the same thing. However Ordnance Survey maps proved me wrong. Yew Tree Farm stood on the western side of Shenley Lane, opposite the present day Shenley Shopping Centre and St David's Church.

I am indebted to Mr and Mrs Alan Chumbley, themselves farmers at Hanbury in Worcestershire, for the following information:

Mr Chumbley's grand-parents, Mr and Mrs Alfred Hodgetts, were the owners of Yew Tree Farm until Mr Hodgett's untimely death from drowning in 1916. As a result of this tragedy the farm had to be sold and Mrs Chumbley and her young children moved to a private house in Weoley Park Road, Selly Oak. A few years later, one of the daughters, Mary, married Mr Philip

Yew Tree Farmhouse.

The Hodgett's Family,
Yew Tree Farm

The Drive, Yew Tree Farm.

120

Chumbley and for some years they lived in Green Meadow Road. Their son, the aforementioned Alan Chumbley, has been kind enough to provide me with a copy of the Bill of Sale for Yew Tree Farm together with sundry photographs of the farmhouse and members of his family.

Following the demolition of the farm in the 1950's roads were constructed and houses and bungalows built to the extreme western boundary of the Bournville Estate, *i.e.* Merritt's Hill, with Meadow Brook Road to the south, Shenley Lane to the east and Long Mynd Road to the north.

Mare and Foal, Yew Tree Farm.

121

Furniture at Eleven o'clock.

KITCHEN.

1 Deal table with extra leaf
2 Two Windsor chairs
3 Fireguard
4 Wringing machine
5 Duplex-burner hanging lamp
6 Sundries
7 Ditto
8 Ditto
9 Ditto

DRAWING ROOM.

10 DRAWING-ROOM SUITE, in satin-walnut, upholstered in tapestry, viz., 6 small chairs and 2 easy chairs and couch
11 Set of tapestry covers
12 Hanging lamp
13 Handsome satin wood overmantel
14 Three corner wall brackets
15 Flower stand
16 Brass cornice pole
17 Square of Brussels carpet
18 Stained deal table
19 Sundries
20 Ditto
21 Ditto

DINING ROOM.

22 Well-made mahogany KNEE-HOLE WRITING DESK, with 2 large drawers and 8 small ditto
23 Mahogany cornice pole, &c.
24 Iron curb with copper rail
25 Fire irons
26 Handsome hanging lamp
27 Sundries

HALL.

28 Hanging lamp

BEDROOM, No. 1.

29 Curb with brass rail
30 Set of fireirons
31 Child's chair
32 Cradle
33 Chair bedstead, with cushions, &c.

BEDROOM. No. 2.

34 Set of iron bedsteads
35 Wool mattress
36 Square of carpeting
37 Stained wash-stand
38 Toilet ware
39 Set of brass window rod fittings
40 Hip bath
41 Small iron bedsteads
42 Wool mattress
43 Painted chest of drawers
44 Well-made wire fire-guard
45 Bracket lamp
46 Mahogany lamp and shade
47 Sundries
48 Ditto
49 Ditto
50 Ditto

DAIRY UTENSILS.

51 Seventeen-gallon milk churn
52 End-over-end oak churn
53 Two buckets
54 STANDARD SEPARATOR, complete
55 Bath tub and boards
56 Three enamelled milk pails
57 Three ditto
58 Three ditto
59 The "Dairy" Table Churn
60 Odd earthenware
61 Ditto
62 Ditto
63 Sundries
64 Ditto
65 Ditto

Implements at Twelve o'(...)

66 Wheelbarrow
67 Ditto
68 Ditto
69 Old iron
70 Ditto
71 Ditto
72 Quantity spouting
73 Quantity converted timber
74 Ditto
75 Ditto
76 Quantity fencing timber
77 Two large doors
78 Small iron gate

178 4½in. wheel cart by Giles
179 4in. ditto
180 4in. ditto
181 WELL-MADE 4 IN. WHEEL LORRY, with crates and sideboard
182 Strong harvest wagon
183 Spring trap
184 Well-made rubber-tyred float
185 Ditto dog cart, with lamps and cushions
186 Ditto   ditto
187 Small governess cart, with rubber tyres
188 QUANTITY RAILWAY SLEEPERS, in 6 lots
189 ABOUT 70 STRONG IRON HURDLES, in lots
190 THIRTY WOOD DITTO, in lots
191 Large wood and galvanized fowl house in orchard
192 Ditto on wheels
193 Lean-to ditto
194 Quantity drain pipes
195 Ditto
196 Ditto
197 Wood and wire fowl run
198 Grindstone and posts

GEARING AND HARNESS.

199 Set of thillers gears
200 Set of long gears
201 Ditto   ditto
202 G.O tackle
203 Part set ditto
204 Odd cart collars
205 Ditto and bridle
206 Set of black trap harness
207 Ditto
208 Odd ditto
209 Riding saddle and bridle
210 Cob-size collar
211 Two ditto
212 Two belly bands
213 Head stall
214 Kicking strap
215 Four horse cloths
216 Pair knee caps
217 Pair pole straps
218 Ditto
219 Sundry harness, about 6 lots
210 Quantity of bits

HORSES.

221 BROWN NAG MARE "Blossom." 15·1 hands, 6 years old, quiet to ride and drive
222 HER PROMISING FILLY FOAL, by Stretton Wonder

PIGS.

223 Four prime quality small bacons
224 Five strong porks
225 Five ditto

SHEEP.

226 Six fat sheep and lambs

CATTLE.

NOTE.—The cattle will be sold at 4.0 o'clock, or as near as catalogue will allow.

227 Hereford cow in milk	1
228 Ditto	2
229 Brindled cow in milk	3
230 Shorthorn cow in milk	4
231 Ditto ditto	5
232 Hereford cow in milk	6
233 Ripe Hereford cow	7
234 Ditto	8
235 Ditto	9
236 Ditto	10
237 Ripe grey cow	11
238 Ripe shorthorn cow	12
239 Ditto Hereford cow	13
240 Ditto Hereford heifer	14
241 Ditto ditto	15
242 Ditto ditto	16
243 Black ditto	17
244 Crossbred ditto	18
245 Hereford ditto	19

POULTRY.

246 About 60 young hens in lots
247 Three cockerels
248 Twenty-two early chickens

Sales Brochure, Yew Tree Farm.

Lower Shenley Farm

BENTLEY'S WORCESTERSHIRE DIRECTORY dated 1841 records William Summerfield, farmer, coal and lime dealer living at Lower Shenley Farm, as is R. Bond.

The Bournville Village Trust *Notes on a visit to farm properties dated August 1935* reports as follows;

Lower Shenley Farm.

The tenant was on the milk round but Mrs Stevenson showed us round the farmhouse. This was re-conditioned at the change of tenancy two years ago and is now kept in excellent condition. The new grates, bathroom and electric light were noted.

We walked up the fields and saw some very good crops of wheat and oats. The land is now very clean and fertile and very different from the condition when the tenant took over.

Lower Shenley Farm is demolished.

Green Meadow School from a demolished Lower Shenley Farmyard.

Shenley Lane at junction with Black Haynes Road.

124

The pool at the back of the farm has sprung a leak and will not hold water.

The new and the old cow-sheds were inspected. The roof of the latter is bad and it will probably be necessary to alter the cow-stalls sometime to comply with modern requirements for clean milk production.

The Yew Tree Farm area was included in development plans by Bournville Village Trust during the 1930's but, as in other areas of The Estate, these had to be delayed, due to war being declared. By the 1950's amended plans were in place and as a result we now have the Shenley Green Shopping Centre, St David's Church, and surrounding houses, maisonettes and flats.

Stock's Wood.

These two pictures were prizewinners in a Bournville Works Photographic Competition in 1908.

Meadow Scene, Bournville.

126

*'Stirchley Street' –
later 'Bournville' Station 1879.*

Day trippers to Bournville 1931.

127

Thorn Road, 1911.

*Graham White lands at
Bournville 1912.*

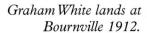

Clerks' Outing, 1917.

Bristol Road, 1930's.

Bristol Road, 1960's.

130

Bournville Schools, 1912.

Bournville Park, 1908.

131

The Green, Bournville, 1910.

The Green, Bournville, 1950's.

Bournville Park with the Park-keeper's shed.

May-Day early 1920's. Assembly of Roy's bakery delivery carts.

133

*Delivery cart belonging to
Mr Shipley, village grocer.*

*Mr Arthur Seaman,
assistant to Mr Shipley, 1920's.*

Sycamore Road at the junction with Maple Road before the Day Continuation Schools were built.

Sycamore Road/Laburnum Road with some of the early Cadbury factory buildings in the fore-ground.

This cottage stood in Oak Tree Lane until the 1960's when it was demolished to make way for the development of Oak Tree House.

136

Cottages nos 12/14 Hay Green Lane with Dame Elizabeth Cadbury School in the background.

Bournville Village from the air, 1920's.

Taken from the School tower in the early 1930's, this is a view of the Bournville Estate.

Bournville Park 1950's.

The Valley Parkway.

140

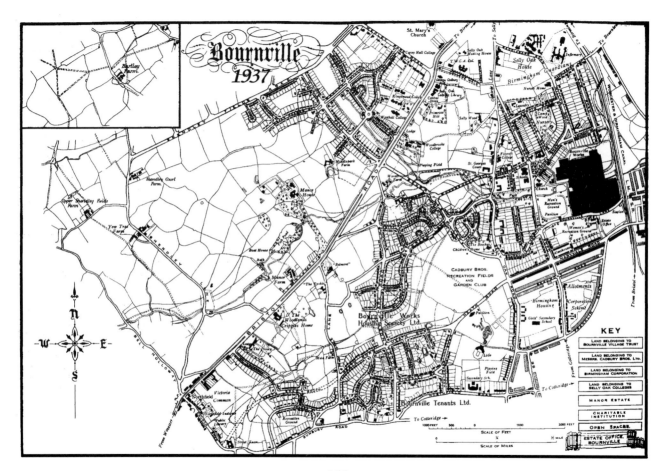

Bournville 1937

KEY

LAND BELONGING TO BOURNVILLE VILLAGE TRUST

LAND BELONGING TO MESSRS. CADBURY BROS. LTD.

LAND BELONGING TO BIRMINGHAM CORPORATION

LAND BELONGING TO SELLY OAK COLLEGES

MANOR ESTATE

CHARITABLE INSTITUTION

OPEN SPACES

ESTATE OFFICE BOURNVILLE

SCALE OF FEET

SCALE OF MILES

141

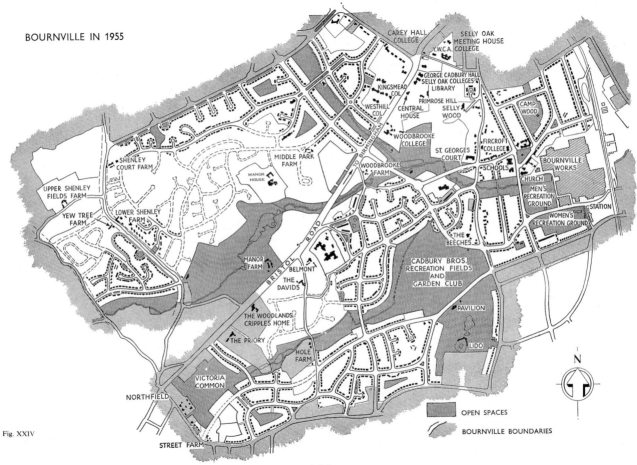

BOURNVILLE IN 1955

CAREY HALL
COLLEGE

SELLY OAK
MEETING HOUSE
Y.W.C.A. COLLEGE

GEORGE CADBURY HALL
SELLY OAK COLLEGES
LIBRARY

KINGSMEAD
COL.

WESTHILL
COL.

CENTRAL
HOUSE

PRIMROSE HILL
SELLY
WOOD

CAMP
WOOD

WOODBROOKE
COLLEGE

FIRCROFT
COLLEGE

ST. GEORGES
COURT

SHENLEY
COURT FARM

MIDDLE PARK
FARM

WOODBROOKE
FARM

SCHOOLS

BOURNVILLE
WORKS

MANOR
HOUSE

UPPER SHENLEY
FIELDS FARM

CHURCH

MEN'S
RECREATION
GROUND

YEW TREE
FARM

LOWER SHENLEY
FARM

STATION

WOMEN'S
RECREATION GROUND

THE
BEECHES

MANOR
FARM

BELMONT

THE
DAVIDS

CADBURY BROS.
RECREATION FIELDS
AND
GARDEN CLUB

THE WOODLANDS
CRIPPLES HOME

PAVILION

THE PRIORY

LIDO

HOLE
FARM

N

VICTORIA
COMMON

NORTHFIELD

OPEN SPACES

BOURNVILLE BOUNDARIES

Fig. XXIV

STREET FARM

TO BIRMINGHAM

BRISTOL ROAD

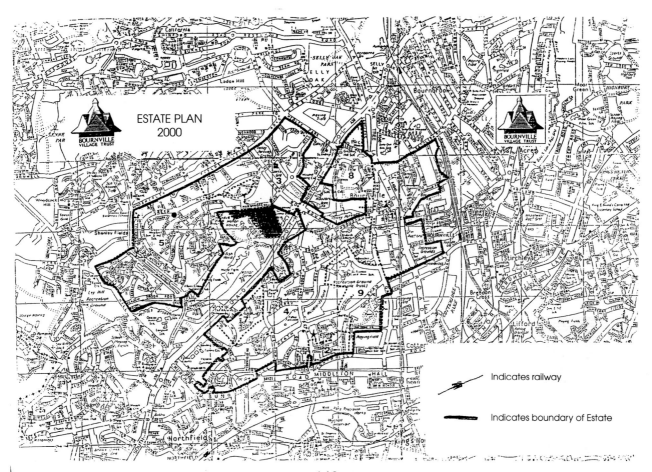

ESTATE PLAN
2000

BOURNVILLE
VILLAGE TRUST

Indicates railway

Indicates boundary of Estate

Conclusion

THIS THEN IS MY INTERPRETATION of the way in which the area now referred to as the Bournville Estate has developed throughout the centuries.

I have relied heavily on the written word of others when dealing with the long ago history of the area and I acknowledge their generosity in allowing me to use quotations from their works.

I am greatly indebted to the various members of families who farmed in the area for the encouragement they have given me. Submitting, as they did, both written accounts and photographs of their life on the farm has helped enormously to bring the latter part of the 19th and first half of the 20th centuries alive.

For all my life I have lived either in the village or on the Weoley Hill Estate, and during that time I have been fortunate enough to make acquaintance with many of those who have striven to make Bournville the picturesque suburb of Birmingham it is today. I not only refer to the many and varied individual people who have served as appointed Bournville Trustees throughout the years, but also to those who, as employees, tenants or private home-owners have striven to implement the wishes of George Cadbury and by so doing can look around and see the fruits of their labours. As I take a break from my writing and view the world outside my window, I cannot help but give thanks for their diligence. May future generations continue along the same path.

Addenda

Weoley Castle and its Owners

Pre 1066 ALWOLD / ALWOLDE / ALFWOLD held the Northfield / Weoley land.

1086 WILLIAM son of ANSCULF.
The manor was later given to William's daughter who married GERVASE PAGANEL. There were no children of the marriage and therefore the manor passed via marriage to Gervase Paganel's sister who married ROGER de SOMERY.

1264 ROGER de SOMERY, who was an ally of Henry III against Simon de Montfort at the battle of LEWES, was granted a Royal licence to build stone walls as fortification.
ROGER de SOMERY died in 1273. His children were inheritors of the estate.

1322 Manor passed to JOAN de SOMERY, a minor, and therefore the Manor was administered by JOHN de HAMPTON for some time.

1327 JOAN married THOMAS de BOTETORT and the BOTETORT family became owners.

1384 JOYCE de BOTETORT married HUGH de BURNELL. There were no children of the marriage.

1386 Sir HUGH de BURNELL was Governor of Bridgnorth Castle. For a time Sir HUGH de BURNELL represented the manor in Parliament, and he was one of those who, in 1399, received Richard II's abdication. Sir HUGH died in 1430. The manor passed to CATHERINE, cousin of JOYCE de BURNELL.

1439 CATHERINE married Sir MAURICE de BERKLEY, and the Manor passed to the BERKLEY family.

1465 MAURICE (son of MAURICE and CATHERINE?) Lord of the Manor.

1495 WILLIAM de BERKLEY son and heir of MAURICE was attainted and forfeited the Manor. It was given to JOHN DUDLEY and afterwards to his grandson and heir EDWARD.

1532 Manor sold to EDWARD SUTTON, Lord DUDLEY.

1536 Manor bought by RICHARD JERVEYS, Sheriff of London.

1586 RICHARD was succeeded by his son THOMAS JERVEYS, who died under suspicious circumstances at the family seat, Butford, nr. Salisbury, leaving a one-year-old son, also THOMAS.

1611 THOMAS JERVEYS junior was knighted by King James I. In 1644 THOMAS JERVEYS succeeded the Duke of Lennox as steward of the Manor of Richmond. THOMAS died in 1654 and was succeeded by his son, Captain THOMAS JERVOISE.

1667 Captain THOMAS JERVOISE had a son, also THOMAS, who had a daughter ELIZABETH. She married SAMUEL CLARKE, son of Sir SAMUEL CLARKE of West Bromwich.

1733 Between this date and 1762 many of the JERVOISE and JERVOISE-CLARKE-JERVOISE family died.

1767 By this time the original JERVOISE line was extinct.

1777 the JERVOISE CLARKE's assumed the surname and arms of JERVOISE by Act of Parliament. The manor remained in their name until 1809.

1809 Weoley Manor was bought by DANIEL LEDSAM, whose wife was SARAH ELIZABETH SODIE of Allesley. They had four children, two of whom died in infancy.

1837 DANIEL LEDSAM died and was succeeded to the Lordship by his nephew JOSEPH FREDERICK LEDSAM. His wife was ELIZABETH ANN ASHTON CODDINGTON.

1861 JOSEPH FREDERICK LEDSAM died, and his eldest surviving son, FREDERICK GEORGE LEDSAM, became Lord of the Manor.

1876 Upon the death of FREDERICK GEORGE LEDSAM the Lordship of the Manor passed to his younger brother, JAMES CODDINGTON LEDSAM. It is believed the loss of his brother deeply affected JAMES CODDINGTON LEDSAM. He is reported to have ended his days almost as a recluse, living in a large house, surrounded by an 8-ft. high brick wall. The house stood where we now have Princethorpe Junior and Infant Schools. He died in 1929.

1930 The executors of JAMES CODDINGTON LEDSAM sold the remainder of Weoley Manor Estate to the Birmingham Corporation and The Weoley Castle Housing Estate was built on the land.

N.B.   ROAD NAMES
ALWOLD road, BOTTETOURT Road, BURNEL Road, CASTLE Road, JERVOISE Road, PAGANEL Road, SOMERY Road, WEOLEY Avenue, WEOLEY CASTLE Road, WEOLEY HILL, WEOLEY PARK Road.

Woodbrooke

The following has been written by Mrs Kathleen Edwards of Bournville.

My parents were in service at Woodbrooke in the late 1890's, having come to Birmingham in search of work – father from a farm-labouring family in Gloucestershire and mother from a coal-mining village in Gloucestershire.

Father, Charles George Compton, was employed in the gardens, which I imagine have changed little over the years, in particular the walled garden and woodland area.

Mother, Annie Elizabeth Yearby, worked in the house on the many jobs involved in the running of a large residence at that time.

I never heard mention of my parents' employers by name. George and Elizabeth M. Cadbury had moved from Woodbrooke to Northfield Manor in 1894, and it has not been possible to find out who occupied Woodbrooke in the years up to 1903 when the College was founded. I understand John and Mabel Barlow lived there for a time while their new house 'Primrose Hill' was completed. It's possible, I suppose, that a skeleton domestic staff cared for the house during those years, while various Quaker families were in residence for short periods. My mother clearly recalled a housekeeper by the name of Mrs Mappelbeck, who obviously occupied a position of some authority.

When they were married in 1899 at St Mary's Parish Church, Selly Oak, my parents were offered accommodation at 'The Lodge', Woodbrooke. A small house, it was situated in what is now the middle of the Bristol Road. By 1907, with three or four children, the family needed more space and moved to Reservoir Road, off Harborne Lane. The two older boys were among the first pupils at the newly-opened Bournville School, while their sister attended the nearer St Mary's Church School until she was able to manage the longer walk to Bournville.

The original Lodge was demolished in the early 1920's, when a piece of Woodbrooke's land was sacrificed for the widening of Griffin's Hill (Bristol Road) to allow for the extension of the Birmingham Corporation Tram Track from Selly Oak to the Lickeys.

Annie Compton, with little formal education, but a lively and enquiring mind, became aware of the Quaker way of life she saw demonstrated around her, and she watched with interest the comings and goings of prominent Friends concerned in the formation and growth of Woodbrooke College.

A further house move took the family to one of the new Bournville Village Trust properties in Selly Oak Road, and it was at this time my mother began attending the evening Fellowship Meetings at Bournville Friends' Meeting House. She eventually applied for membership and was accepted in 1927.

Among her memories of Woodbrooke was the building, in 1906, of 'Holland House', so named because of the large influx of Dutch students who came to hear Dr Rendel Harris, a distinguished orientalist and theologian. Like Professor Herbert G. Wood, he had chosen to take up a post on the College tutorial staff rather than one at Leyden in Holland.

In May 1999 I attended a service at St Mary's Church in commemoration of my parents' 100th wedding anniversary and tried to imagine the area a century earlier – fields, farms, a few big houses, some horse-drawn vehicles, farm carts, a brougham with a liveried coachman perhaps? My sister, towards the end of her long life, clearly remembered the thrill of an occasional ride in the latter.

Memories of Mr Fred Meredith, b. 1902

The Northfield Society 1983 occasional paper no. 14 entitled *Down Memory Lane,* is made up of a collection of memories (gathered by Leonard G. Day in 1980) and recalled by people who lived in the Northfield area during the first half of the 20th century. One of the contributors was a Mr Fred Meredith. As a postscript to the many and varied accounts of life on a farm at that time, I am pleased to be able to quote from Mr Meredith's memoirs.

Born near Knighton, Fred Meredith was brought, at the age of 13, to The Cottage, Woodcock Lane, Bartley Green, where he lived until 1932. The cottage stood in the grounds of Shenley Cottage Homes where Mr Meredith's father was maintenance engineer.

Fred Meredith goes on to say

> The pre-World War I period were hungry days for some folk. Poaching and fowl stealing went on at night. I became aware that men were working in Cromwell Lane and went out to discover what they were doing. They had two long canes similar to those used by groundsmen on the golf course. Attached to these was fine netting. One man held the huge net up to the hedge. Another held a lamp behind the netting, and two more men were beating the hedge from the other side for sparrows or whatever else was resting for the night. In those days no one would complain about this as sparrows were considered a pest, and we were taught how to trap them with a riddle and a long string. We also used small bore guns or air rifles. I was never any good with a riddle and lost the desire to shoot early in life.

Mr Meredith goes on to mention various characters he remembers, such as William Kinder, a chimney sweep who, it is said, also made wooden false teeth; William Young, blacksmith; Thomas Inston the wheelwright; Fletcher who had a threshing machine; Hadley the hedge-layer and hay trusser; Brett the haulier and pea and beanstick merchant.

When asked about the Lord of the Manor, Fred Meredith said

> The last of the Ledsams built himself a large house at the corner of what is now Marston Road and Shenley Lane (occupied now by St Gabriel's Church). That was about 1903. The house was walled in on three sides, leaving only the front exposed, and, at the western side, a private, gated drive ran all the way to what is now the main entrance to Lodge Hill Cemetery. This was called The Postman's Road, because he had a key to the gate which enabled him to deliver the letters to the farm which lay in the fields some distance from the lane. . . . The avenue of trees down Princethorpe Road are a remnant of the old Postman's Road. Ledsam called his house 'Shendley' – why he added the 'd' I do not know. Hadley was the man who ran the farm.

Mr Meredith continues:

> As a boy I helped drive cattle and sheep along to Kings Norton market without the aid of dogs – what an adventure! They split up twice and got away towards Cadbury's Manor from Shenley Lane. They then strayed across the cricket field – where Innage Road is now – and we were not able to turn them until we reached the pools behind Garland's Farm. After this we had to contend with all the carriage gateways down Middleton Hall Road. Although we were only four in number we managed to get to market on time with about a dozen fat cattle and 20 sheep. These sheep were a new venture and a failure. The fences at the farm were not up to standard for sheep and every morning they were missing. They provided my first job as a schoolboy, when I had to get up early and get them home. They were such a bother, Jim Ward gave them best and put them to market.
>
> My next job, a Saturday part-time one, was at Yew Tree Farm. Using a hoe in the large garden and among the swedes in season, I had to line up with the men. My reward was 1/3d a day plus bread and cheese and milk at the house at 11 o'clock. When I left school at 14, I had

three weeks at the farm at 7/6d weekly plus my elevenses. Then I worked at Cadbury's at 8/- per week with a 50% increase after the first month.

Extracts from the memories of Herbert F. Davey, written in 1987

The estate of Colonel Stocks of Bournbrook Hall came on the market in 1878. Apart from the Hall and one cottage, it was literally a green field site of 14 acres and was acquired by Richard and George Cadbury at auction. Records show that on 4th March 1879, the brothers submitted plan no. 347 (architect, J B. Williams) for building a 'Cocoa and Chocolate Manufactory on land purchased from the executors of Colonel Stocks'.

In September 1906, my family moved from Surrey to Bournville. I was four years old. I remember seeing one of the last steam trams running in Birmingham. At that time, Bournville village was not completed. There was no Woodbrooke Road and the park was still a field. Housebuilding in Elm Road was incomplete, the Post Office was no. 84 Linden Road and there were only six shops on The Green. Lloyds Bank and adjoining shops were built later. In 1906, Bournville School was opened, and Herbert Austin started making motor cars at Longbridge.

Hay Green Lane was completely in the country with Walker's Farm and Sheward's Farm. Woodlands Park Road had been cut but grass and weeds grew through the metalled surface – the only house was Middleton Hall Farm, at the corner of Bunbury Road.

There were two large rookeries, one in the Girls' Grounds and one in Camp Wood – the noise of rooks settling on their nests created a countryside atmosphere.

My father was appointed Paper Buyer in the Buying office of Cadbury Brothers in 1906. One of my earliest recollections is of attending a summer party at the Dell – the residence of Mr E. S. Thackeray

– head of the Buying Office. The Dell (the gardens of which ran down to Bournville Park) became Fircroft College and is now the Bournville Village Trust Offices.

Another treat to which I and my sister looked forward was a visit to Town. We travelled by train and this meant walking to Bournville Station from our home, 121 Bournville Lane. On our way we passed Bournbrook Hall, in the Girls' Recreation Grounds, the lawns of which ran right down to the lane. On the left we passed a few cottages with their gardens fronting onto the lane. (This is where we now have the Dining rooms and Concert Hall block.) These cottages were built 16 years before the village. . . .

We are brought nearer to the completion of the model village by an extract from the memoirs of Dame Elizabeth Cadbury recorded in 1948 when she celebrated her 90th birthday.

> When I first came to Birmingham and we were living at Woodbrooke, I would walk morning by morning with my husband through the fields and farmland, between our home and the Works, planning how a village could be developed, where the roads should run and the type of cottages and buildings.

This would be soon after her marriage in 1888 when George Cadbury was 48 and she was 30.

My father-in-law, Robert Quinton, whose family home was 142 Oak Tree Lane, Selly Oak, was born in 1870 – nine years before Richard and George Cadbury moved their business from Bridge Street. He recalled that, when he was a boy, there were large double gates at the entrance to Stock's Drive, just outside his front garden. There is a photograph showing the tree-lined stretch of the first 500 yards of this drive which would correspond to Linden Road up to the junction with Acacia Road. The drive then dropped down through fields to the brook and up to Bournbrook Hall.

In the course of digging the foundations of houses in Sycamore Road some past history of the neighbourhood was revealed. The workmen unearthed hundreds of spent bullets. They were duly submitted to a Museum and were declared to be the type used in the Civil War. Rumour has it that soldiers of an army in the Civil War (Royalist or Cromwell's is not known) were garrisoned on a site in the vicinity of old Bournbrook Hall. One assumes the nicely sheltered Sycamore Road site was an ideal spot for shooting practice.

Street Farm

The following is a compilation of memories of Street Farm as recalled by Roger Wallbank and Meriel Hunt (neé Manasseh), who, as children during the 30's and early 40's, lived in Norman Road and Bunbury Road respectively. Roger writes;

> Meriel says the farm in Bunbury Road was Field's Farm (or possibly Fields' Farm). To get to the farmhouse we would walk up Norman Road, cross Bunbury road and walk a little way towards the Bristol Road. The farmhouse was on the right and as I remember it, its front wall was up to the pavement. The Fields had a daughter – Nelly – from whom one bought cream. The charge was ninepence for a jugfull, irrespective of the size of the jug! All I can remember is tagging along with my sister and carrying a china jug with a cover for keeping off the flies, the cover being a circle of white handkerchief material with glass beads of different colours attached to it by threads and serving to hold the cover in place on the top of the jug.
>
> Meriel remembers that before the Recreation Ground was built behind their house in Bunbury Road, there was a field in which cows grazed. Perhaps they belonged to Field's Farm. She remembers that on one occasion cows from the field broke into their garden and smashed her father's cold-frames.
>
> I myself remember Innage Road being cut through to Bunbury Road and riding on my fairy-cycle over heaps of sand and gravel left in the roadway as the road was being built. And I well remember the 'Rec' and the tennis courts; we spent a lot of time playing there.

Meriel also recalls the farm down Hole Lane. This was presumably Hole Farm. I think that the cowman was Mr Lilwall (?spelling). He was certainly our milkman and used to come round each morning with his horse-drawn dray loaded with churns of milk. This he doled out at the back door using one-pint and half-pint 'dippers' – measures that had bent handles that hung on the rim of the churn. The horse knew at which houses to stop and walked from one house to the next when given the word. Mr Lilwall wore leather gaiters, and I remember him coming into the hall one Christmas and drinking a glass of sherry, having first raised his glass to the Christmas Tree.

Occasionally when we (the local pack of children) went down to the farm Mr Lilwall would be tipping the milk into the separator (I think it was an Alfa-Laval machine). He would then turn the handle and the top would spin round very fast and bring about the separation of the cream from the milk. Once or twice I was allowed to turn the handle myself and can remember the tremendous force exerted on one's hands due to the momentum of the spinning mechanism.

Meriel, however, said that at one time she kept a horse at the farm and that the farm was owned by a 'Miss something'. She also said that there was a fierce servant woman there.

Continuing, Roger writes;

When we lived in Norman Road (1930-1939) there was a lot of open land in the neighbourhood that must once have been farmland. Almost opposite our house, for example, there was the beginning (perhaps 20 yards) of road that ended immediately in land used as a games field. I seem to recall rugger-posts there. Then, as I walked along Bunbury Road to Brunnaker School in Northfield Road, there was a lot of open space on the right. The last house before that – one with a tall gable with a date on it – belonged to the Drakes. After that it was open land until Pope's Lane. Down by Northfield station there were fields. And down Bell Hill, of course, there it was all open land for miles and a good place for picnics.

Roger concludes by saying;

Some of what I have said above is from Meriel and some from me. Whether either of us has a perfect memory for what happened more than 60 years ago, I rather doubt; but on the whole I expect that what I have written is true.

The Manor Farm

The following was written by Mr George Parsons.

I was born in Thorn Road, Bournville, in one of those houses which faces Bournville Park at the bottom of the road. It was really a splendid place in which to grow up although I doubt whether my friends and I appreciated our good fortune. The park was well used in those days with the tennis courts and bowling green in full use during the Summer months. My friends and I spent a good deal of our time in the park and I fear we must have been a sore trial to the park-keeper and his assistants.

From the age of five I attended Dr Archibald's graded Sunday School which took over the whole of Bournville Schools, the Ruskin Hall and the Lofts which used to stand behind the Old Farm Inn on the corner of Bournville Lane and Linden Road. The Sunday School was closely connected with the Bournville Friends' Meeting on Bournville Green.

I progressed through the various departments of the Sunday School until, in my late teens, I reached the Seniors at the Lofts under the tutelage of the excellent Wilfred Beswick. There were numerous activities in addition to the Sunday Meeting; a Youth Club met on Thursday evenings and, on some of the Summer weekends, Wilfred would take us to camp at the Manor Farm on the Bristol Road. On the Sunday mornings, some of us at least would cycle down to Bournville Friends' Meeting.

So it was on that first weekend of September 1939. The weather was beautiful and we camped at the Manor Farm, aware of the gathering war clouds. At Bournville Meeting, one Friend stayed out to listen to the Prime Minister's speech on the radio and came in to tell us that war had been declared.

I had already decided that I would follow the pacifist path and that, if possible, I would join the Friends' Ambulance Unit, which had done such good work in the 1914-18 war, if it should be re-activated. I took immediate steps and found that the new F.A.U. was in the process of formation largely through the efforts of Paul Cadbury and Arnold Rowntree. I was accepted for the first training camp which was to be held at the Manor Farm. So I reported there on the 28th September, less than a month after we had camped there with the Sunday School.

This was rather different though. There were 60 of us and instead of tents in the fields we slept in bunkhouses which had been converted from the stables round the yard. I slept in the two storey bunkhouse at the end of the yard and, for some reason, I was appointed one of the two buglers although I had never blown a bugle before. One of my tasks was to sleep with an alarm clock set for 6.30 a.m. when I would crawl from my bunk and blow the bugle through a kind of window in the wall. On a recent visit to the Manor Farm, the outline of the window was still there although it had been bricked in.

On arising, first of all everyone had to run up the hill on the Bristol Road as far as the *Travellers' Rest* in Northfield and back again, a distance of, I suppose, about a mile. Then it was breakfast in the large barn where we took all our meals and had our lectures. The members of each bunkhouse took it in turns to be on kitchen duty and the food was surprisingly edible considering that few of us had any experience of cooking.

I think I was a little surprised at how much square bashing and route marching there was, but thanks to lectures by Dr Rutter an elderly local medico and of Sister Gibbs from the surgery at Bournville Works, we acquired a good deal of medical knowledge. We learned motor mechanics and air raid precautions too. There were night operations when Paul Cadbury would arrive on his motorbike and sidecar in the small hours of the morning and turn us out to hunt for planted 'casualties' over the fields in the darkness. Just before the end of our stay, we organised a dance in the barn to which members invited some of the local young ladies they had taken up with during the camp. For a year or two I had been running a little dance band in my spare time and we provided the music.

The camp lasted for six weeks during which time a disparate group of young men from differing backgrounds drew together into a cohesive unit. We had to vacate the Manor Farm because it was needed for the second training camp. I think we had visualised setting off for France to drive ambulances but there was no call for this and we were sent to work in hospitals in London for the time being.

Towards the end of 1940 an opportunity arose for the F.A.U. to send a party of 40 to China to carry out relief and ambulance work made necessary by the Sino-Japanese war. Early in 1941 we assembled at the Manor Farm where we were tutored in Mandarin Chinese by Dr Simon from the School of Oriental Studies in London and by Hsiao Chen, an expatriate Chinese who had been a newspaper editor in Beijing. We had an extensive course in motor mechanics and lorry driving and learned a good deal about unpleasant tropical diseases.

The Manor Farm had changed little since our previous occupation although this time I was quartered in one of the single-story bunkhouses. I remember there were several air raids while we were there and, on one particular night, two houses in Bournville Lane by the Valley Pool were hit by delayed action bombs and the following morning they were destroyed. Although much of the routine was similar to that of the first camp in 1939, I do not recall that we had to do the morning run up to Northfield.

After six weeks the Manor Farm was required for yet another training camp and we moved to a Youth Hostel in London to complete our training. Because of wartime shipping difficulties we had to leave for China in small parties and I sailed out in August 1941. The account of our adventures in China has no place here; suffice to say that it was six years before I returned. I think that while we were away, all of us kept our memories of the times we had spent at the Manor Farm.